# Enthusiastic Response to Inspired Philanthropy

*Inspired Philanthropy* invites a diverse spectrum of donors, development staff, activists, and foundation and investment professionals to take time to envision and build the world they want to live in. Build a bridge with someone you know through the gift of this workbook and the dialogue it will foster.

    —TERRY ODENDAHL, Executive Director, National Network of Grantmakers and author of *Charity Begins at Home*

*Inspired Philanthropy* is an excellent resource for young people who want to become better informed and more strategic givers.

    —TRACY HEWAT, Comfort Zone

A most practical and useful giving guide for donors interested in social change issues.

    —DOT RIDINGS, President and CEO, Council on Foundations

As a churchman privileged to read the final draft of this very inspiring and practical guidebook, I found myself saying "Wow!" This is the very answer we in the pulpit and pew alike have needed and been searching for to help revitalize an authentic sense of Christian discipleship and stewardship.

    —DON McCLANEN, Founder, The Ministry of Money

It's time for this book. As someone has said, it's time to raise less corn and more hell.

    —KAREN SUSAN YOUNG, Youth on Board

Money—we need to talk about it and we need to redistribute it. Some of that redistribution comes through our charitable giving. This book proposes a disciplined, strategic planning process for giving, so that we can experience maximum social change for our contributions. Read it, use it, and give to a friend.

    —RINKU SEN, Co-director, Center for Third World Organizing

# Inspired Philanthropy

## Creating a Giving Plan

# Inspired Philanthropy

## Creating a Giving Plan

### A WORKBOOK

by Tracy Gary & Melissa Kohner

**EDITED BY NANCY ADESS**

**Chardon Press**
BERKELEY, CA

A full set of the exercises in this book is available as overheads from Chardon Press for $50 (includes tax and first-class mailing). A copy of the Giving Plan form can be downloaded at www.chardonpress.com.

A portion of net proceeds from this book benefits organizations working for inspired philanthropy. We welcome your suggestions for future editions. Contact the authors at: tracygary1@aol.com; or msk4@aol.com.

Library of Congress Catalog Card Number: 98-73290
ISBN 1-890759-03-1

Cover and book design by Cici Kinsman, C$^2$ Graphics, Oakland, CA
Editing by Nancy Adess

Printed in the United States of America

Printed on recycled paper with soy ink.

Chardon Press
P.O. Box 11607
Berkeley, California 94712
(510) 704-8714
www.chardonpress.com

10 9 8 7 6 5 4 3 2 1

**SOURCES:**

PAGE ix: "The Power of Doing Good," by Suze Orman, reprinted with permission from *Currency* (Condé Nast Publications, 1998).

PAGE 3: Statistics from *Giving and Volunteering 1994* (Independent Sector).

PAGE 7: *The Nonprofit Almanac*, 1996–1997 edition (Independent Sector).

PAGE 8: Charts and statistics: *Giving USA 1998* (AAFRC Trust for Philanthropy).

PAGE 9: "We Grew Together, We Grew Apart" charts courtesy of United for a Fair Economy.

PAGE 32: Data on wealth and income: *Current Population Survey*, U.S. Census Bureau, 1996; *Survey of Consumer Finances*, 1992 and 1995, Federal Reserve Bank (provided by United for a Fair Economy); University of Michigan, Institute for Social Research.

PAGE 33: Growth of alternative workplace giving funds: *Charity in the Workplace* (National Committee for Responsive Philanthropy, 1997).

PAGE 41: "The Volunteer's Rights and Responsibilities" courtesy of San Francisco Volunteer Center.

APPENDIX A: "Donor Bill of Rights" developed by AAFRC, AHP, CASE, and NSFRE.

# Contents

# Exercises and Worksheets

# The Power of Doing Good

## Giving to a worthy cause is worth more than you know

BY SUZE ORMAN

When charitable requests come in the mail, making a pitch for your support to stop global warming, prevent cancer, fund a local food bank or preserve a nature conservancy, do you read the letters? Throw them away with the supermarket circulars? Or do you give as much as you can?

There are scores of good causes, and many of us feel we can't afford to give to all—or any. The larger view suggests that we can't afford not to give to some. There's a moral component to the issue, of course, and everyone has to decide privately how much he or she owes the world. But there's another factor to consider, one that's not often mentioned. When you donate money to a cause you believe in, you're giving yourself the gift of power.

Familiar scene: You're sitting in front of a stack of monthly bills, writing checks and watching your balance shrink. You come upon an envelope from an organization that supports a charity you care about, or maybe a cause you've given to before, when you felt flusher, or a group whose work you've always admired. Hard-pressed this month, you toss the envelope away, gather up your paid bills, head for the mailbox and set out to run some errands. You feel depleted.

Let's play it another way. While writing checks, you discover an envelope you know contains a worthy plea and, instead of throwing it away, you open it, read the letter and write another check—for $25 or $100; the amount doesn't matter as long as it won't break the bank. As soon as you've signed your name, the light dawns: Hey, come to think of it, you can spare a little money this month. Later, when you head out to pick up the kids from their soccer game, you're lighter on your feet—having discovered new resources of both good fellowship and funds, you're a little less pressured. You're buoyant, proud. Confident, curious. Ready to give and receive. And that's when wealth of all kinds comes your way.

It's really this simple: By giving, you become the receiver of gifts—not the smallest of which is an acquaintance with your own power of choice and your freedom to exercise it for the good.

# Publisher's Note

Chardon Press is proud to be partners with Tracy Gary and Melissa Kohner in publishing this book. The principles of being thoughtful and systematic in your giving and of giving a percentage of your income, regardless of how much or how little money that turns out to be, have long been put forward by religious institutions. The idea of seeing your giving as a critical vehicle in shaping social justice has been added as a variation on this theme by people like Tracy—who helped initiate the first locally based women's foundation, Resourceful Women and other organizations—and the young inheritors who founded the Funding Exchange twenty years ago.

Since then, many people have embroidered this idea into the variety of formats it has today, including nontraditional foundations, alternative workplace giving programs and community loan funds, to name just a few.

Now, for the first time, there is this practical guide for how each individual can do the thinking and planning that givers must do if their donations are to advance the kind of social change they desire. Ultimately, the successful functioning of nonprofits depends on thoughtful donors.

We know that seven out of ten adults in America give away money to nonprofits. That makes us an extremely generous country. These 70 percent of Americans—a far greater percentage than Americans who vote—parted with more than $140 billion in 1997. This enormous amount of money has begun to create a very different world. In work on a multitude of issues, from women's rights to stopping nuclear power plants to creating a domestic violence movement to gay liberation and the victories of the farmworkers, money has been a key factor. As George Pillsbury says, "Money alone cannot buy social change, but without money, there will be no change."

Many people, however, cannot remember why they give money where they do, except that someone asked them. There is nothing inherently wrong with giving spontaneously in response to requests. But I have learned from Tracy and Melissa that impulsive giving is not good stewardship of resources, probably does not promote the deepest values of the donor, and rewards only asking rather than solid work.

After reading this book and doing the exercises described, I think most of us will reserve a small amount of money to give away simply because we are asked, but will use more of the precious resource of our money to further our dreams for a better world.

This book challenges those millions of us who give away money to ask some larger questions about that giving. The answers to these questions will lead to more thoughtful and strategic giving to counter the basic social inequalities of our nation.

By thinking about our voluntary giving, we are forced to think about how we use all of our money, that is, about lifestyle and consumption. These questions lead to another that is implicit in the discussion—the question of our mandatory giving, known as taxes.

I am constantly struck by Americans' resentment of government taxes, a resentment that tends to cross the traditional political lines of left and right. By way of contrast, in Toronto recently I saw a woman standing on a busy street corner asking people to send postcards (which she provided) petitioning the provincial government not to lower taxes at the expense of Canadian relief and foreign aid. People were lined up to sign the postcards! The lesson is this: people in social democracies see taxes as important and necessary and are less likely to resent paying them.

We who believe in justice must raise questions about the uses of our taxes as well as about the uses of traditional private philanthropy. The questions for both institutions—government and philanthropy—largely revolve around the role of government, because the nonprofit sector parallels the governmental sector and is able to function because the government allows it certain tax advantages.

A sampling of the questions that must be asked are:

- Why can't everyone deduct their charitable gifts when determining their income tax? (Now, only the 30 percent who exceed the standard deduction and itemize their taxes receive any tax relief for their giving. Since middle-class, working-class and poor families give the most money away, the vast majority of donations provide no tax benefit to the giver.)

- What is the role of taxes? If, as we are taught, one of the purposes of taxes is to equalize wealth to some extent, why do some people have so much money and so many more have so little?

- How much should a person be able to inherit? Why shouldn't there be a 100 percent inheritance tax on estates over a certain size? Why should anyone be able to accumulate massive amounts of wealth and keep it in their

family for generation after generation?

- Why is most tax money spent on the military when we are not at war with anyone and have no real enemies? Why are we spending more money on arms than the next ten armed nations put together?

Questions about taxes will raise even larger questions, and by now the questions will be nontraditional. For example, instead of asking the very big question, "Why does the richest nation on earth have so many of its people living in poverty?" the questions would be:

- Why does the United States have any people living in poverty at all?

- Why don't we stop talking about the minimum wage and set a maximum wage? (United for a Fair Economy has suggested that no person in a corporation earn more than ten times the person paid the least. This would force wages up at the bottom end and down at the top.)

- Why does the U.S. spend any money at all developing new weapons when the ones we have will destroy the whole earth many times over?

- What is government's role in providing social services, health care, housing and education? Are these activities really the appropriate domains of private nonprofits?

- How can we change our culture so that having money to buy things ceases to be our national obsession?

And so on.

The question of how I can make a difference with my giving, multiplied by millions of people asking it, will lead to asking these larger questions. And by using our charitable dollars strategically and systematically to create progressive social change, we will finally be able to demand big answers to our big questions—revolutionary solutions that will allow all to truly experience the right to life, liberty and the pursuit of happiness.

# Preface

**TRACY GARY**

In my early twenties, I was lucky enough to inherit a trust from my parents. With it came a message from my great grandfather, "Do something for the city, the country, the community in which you live." This message, along with the exuberant example of my parents' giving and community work—this year marks, for instance, the 50th year my mother has volunteered for the Boys Club of New York—moved me to take my responsibilities as a wealthy person very seriously.

In my twenties I worked and volunteered for a variety of diverse organizations in San Francisco (a children's home, a hospital, the probation department, the public defender, American Friends Service Committee and the Interfaith Committee on Corporate Responsibility), learning about the nonprofit world. I also hooked up with a new foundation in San Francisco, the Vanguard Public Foundation, and here, as well as at my work with the San Francisco Women's Building and Women's Foundation, my real political education began. Between 1975 and 1985, I had the good fortune to visit more than 350 nonprofits on behalf of the foundations and community groups that I worked with.

Seeing the dreams, talent and capacity of these activists moved me to want to give more of my own money, time and resources. I decided not only to become public about being a donor, but to tell other wealthy and nonwealthy people about all that I was learning and seeing and to try to get more of them involved. I have spent from 1983 to the present doing just that, through founding Resourceful Women and through public speaking and consultation with donors and groups.

Now, a quarter of a century later, by helping start more than 12 nonprofits and participating on more than 28 boards, I have been part of growing a movement of caring wealthy donors and activists working for societal change. Along the way, I have intentionally given away three-fourths of the money I inherited. My sense of real abundance has come through that giving.

At the height of my giving I was receiving requests from more than 700 groups a year. Unlike my parents, who are very organized about their philanthropy, as a younger donor I was not so organized, and found myself bouncing around from project to project, reacting to whatever came along. I came to realize that there was not only a personal consequence to my disorganization, but that it also affected others when I couldn't find proposals sent to me, or wasn't sure if there was any logic to supporting one project over another. I needed to refine my methods.

I had noticed that foundations had guidelines and statements of purpose or missions for their work. As a result, they knew what they wanted to fund year by year, and groups saved countless hours by knowing the foundation's priorities. Following their example, I began to put my own vision for my work into words, stating what my dreams were and refining them in a manner that could be shared. This process gave me added energy and the focus to find partners for my work.

Creating a giving plan has been a tool not just to help organize my mail and have a response to those who ask me for support, but to bring to light what my own consciousness and intuition would have me prioritize given the needs around me.

During the years of sharing this process with many activists and donors, I have seen thousands of men and women transformed through just taking time to be in better balance between reflection, vision and their actions. And I have seen them begin to share some of the joy I have experienced working in partnership with community funding panels and activists to strengthen society through non-profit activity.

I have also seen the remarkable gap that exists between people's stated desires for societal change and their irregular practices at contributing to making that change. This book is dedicated to helping us all bridge that gap in order to affect the more compelling gap that calls us to action—that of the coexistence of great wealth alongside great suffering in our country and the world. Thinking about our participation as donors—at whatever financial level—I am convinced will help create a more compassionate world for ourselves and the planet.

As Adrienne Rich has written:

> My heart is torn by all I cannot save.
> So much has been destroyed.
> I have to cast my lot
> With those who day after day
> Perversely,
> With no extraordinary power,
> Reconstitute the world.

## MELISSA KOHNER

As one of the generation born in the late 1960s, I have come to philanthropy through neither my mother's view of "doing good works" and "leaving the world a better place" nor that of those who in the 1960s felt a need to deconstruct the system. Instead, I simply was excited early on by work being done on issues I really cared about. I felt so strongly about these issues that I wanted to be part of the work. I took to the streets and went to my checkbook.

Those who analyze these things say that my generation is more serious and concerned about our economic future than previous generations. We are concerned about supporting ourselves, including securing health insurance, paying off student loans, and building careers that can support a family.

So perhaps it is this sober and serious view of the economy and my own role in it that has led me to try to reconcile the relationship between the fickle and unaccountable individual donor and the income that nonprofits need to survive. Giving and fundraising exist in a culture where we are mostly too polite, uncomfortable to ask for money directly; giving is such a random act that nonprofits ask twenty people who care about an issue in order to get one donation towards it.

Religious institutions are so successful in raising money because the collection plate keeps coming around. There it is: you give. Like many, my first early donation was a dollar or two into a collection plate. And it was from that collection plate that I understood that this was how the church kept itself in this building. But for other nonprofits, we must be much more decisive. The appeals come in the mail—what do we want to support?

Thinking ahead of time about what you're committed to and what you want to give to commits you to accomplishing a goal; following a giving plan means engaging in a relationship with nonprofits. Putting your values and mission and commitment on paper challenges you to be as serious about your giving as nonprofits are in needing your support. Most important, it holds you accountable to giving of yourself and your money.

In the last several years I've conducted workshops for other donors on creating giving plans. There, I've seen people who were at best feeling ineffective and ambivalent about giving money, through the process of the workshops uncover clear, impassioned and strategic goals for the world. They leave with much more joy, and with commitment to giving more.

I hope this workbook provides the tools that more people can use in creating their giving plans. Consciousness of our own role and our collective roles in shaping the direction of our society is one solution to the gap between the relationship between nonprofits' needs and donors' giving.

I've gotten restless hearing so much conjecture from those who study philanthropy about where the money needs to come from and how to raise it.

Here is a tool and an answer for everyone.

# Acknowledgments

We join many people who teach and model strategic philanthropy and volunteerism. We offer this workbook in the spirit of all of our collective work.

For allowing us to quote them or draw directly from their stories and inspiring work we thank Angeles Arrien, Harriet Barlow, Miven Booth Trageser, Frank and Ruth Butler, Ralph and Jean Davis, Barbara Dobkin, Marta Drury, Michal Feder, Deb Furry, Greg Garvan, Si Kahn, Peter Karoff, Tatjana Loh, Doug Malcolm, Tracey Minkin, Cate Muther, Margaret E. Olsen, M.D., Suze Orman, Joan Peterson, Steve Paprocki, Michele Prichard, Adrienne Rich, Sarah Silber, Marilyn Stern, Eve Stern, Brad Swift, Chet Tchozewski, Marion Weber, Mike and Janet Valder, and Léonie Walker.

The following organizations allowed us to quote from their materials: AAFRC Trust for Philanthropy, Condé Nast, Grassroots Leadership, Impact Project, Independent Sector, Jewish Fund for Justice, Ma'yan, National Committee for Responsive Philanthropy, National Network of Grantmakers, The Philanthropic Initiative, United for a Fair Economy and the Volunteer Bureau of America.

We are indebted to Margaret Foster, Sue Hoffman, Jenny Ladd, John Levy, Christopher Mogil, Anne Slepian, Mila Visser 't Hooft, Lynn Fiske Watts, and Speed Weed for reading and commenting extensively on drafts and to Michal Feder and Deanne Stone for early coaching and editing. A special thank you goes to Christopher Mogil and Anne Slepian for shaping and fine-tuning the exercises. Joan Fischer and Cheryl Altinkemer also contributed exercises developed in their work with alumni associations.

Paula Ross contributed graceful and creative editing and writing at a key point. Nancy Adess' extraordinary editing, consistent energy and good humor were indispensable to the creation of this workbook, as well as Cici Kinsman's inspired design work and endless patience.

Thank you also to Jenny Bernstein, Susan Beyrle, Frances Bowles, Ames Cushing, the members of the Donor Organizer's Network, Andrea Kaminski at The Women's Philanthropy Institute, the Institute of Noetic Sciences, Laura Loescher, The Northern California Community Loan Fund, Ellen Remmer at The Philanthropic Initiative, Andy Robinson and The Shefa Fund.

We owe our gratitude to Kim Klein and Stephanie Roth of Chardon Press for bringing this workbook to print and for their important contributions to the world.

Thank you to Liberty Hill Foundation which, through its stewardship with donors, was a learning laboratory for this workbook. Resourceful Women, through its groundbreaking work with women donors and its extraordinary members, provided much of the background for this workbook.

Finally, thank you to Diane Foster and Linda Welter for their support, warm food, great ideas and understanding of late hours and long faxes.

# Introduction

When was the last time you gave money or time to a cause knowing that it spoke directly to one of your most treasured dreams?

When was the last time you gave money to a cause and felt confident it was being used wisely—that it would make a difference, help improve the world?

Do you wonder if your donations are really having the impact you wish for? Or how you can be sure that you're putting your resources in the "right place"?

If you've given any amount of time or money for a good cause, or thought about doing so, this book is for you. Yes, you—not just people who see themselves as major donors or philanthropists. In fact you may be among those who give time and money but you may not consider yourself a "donor" at all, thinking that philanthropy is something only wealthy people do.

But if you've given away any amount of money—from a dollar to buy a raffle ticket for your local senior center to thousands of dollars to a favorite charity—or volunteered any amount of time—from a few hours a year as an election polling place monitor to several hours each month on a crisis hotline, from serving meals in a church kitchen to serving on the board of a nonprofit organization, this book is for you.

Why? Because if you're like most givers, you have a deep desire to be engaged in helping others and in making the world a better place. But, like most givers, you may not have thought systematically about whether the resources you give are truly being used as effectively as possible and whether they reflect your own personal philosophy and priorities.

Why does the idea of focusing on our giving, of taking some time to organize it and think through our intentions, so often meet with resistance? In an article in the *Grassroots Fundraising Journal* called "The Why and How of Personal Giving Plans," Steve Paprocki pinpoints three reasons that individual giving is disorganized: 1) individual donors are ashamed of the little amount they give and don't want to talk about it; 2) donors are disillusioned about the effectiveness of charities and have no idea how to establish a well-informed and well-organized giving plan; and 3) people are overwhelmed with the sheer number of requests they receive, many appearing similar. We would add a further hesitation: many people are unsure of how much they can afford to give away.

If you identify with any of these reasons for not planning your giving before now, you're not alone. By the time you've reached the end of this workbook, you'll have left them far behind.

This book will help you make your giving more meaningful for yourself and have more impact. We believe that creating a giving plan, as we outline in this workbook, will not only make you a more effective giver, it will make you an inspired giver. When you're confident in choosing where to put your resources you will be free of the doubts and questions you may have today about the effectiveness of your giving.

*Inspired Philanthropy: Creating a Giving Plan* has grown out of more than ten years of experience working with people who give. In our work with educational organizations like Resourceful Women in California and our consultation with the donors, staffs and boards of nonprofit organizations throughout the country, and with members of national funding networks such as The Funding Exchange and the National Network of Grantmakers, we have stressed the importance of matching one's giving with one's passion and of organizations finding donors who can become true partners in their work.

In this workbook, you'll find that we ask you to think about your deepest hopes for a just world, how to have impact in creating change, and where you can find your place in working for that world.

## WHY GIVE? TRADITIONAL AND PROGRESSIVE PHILANTHROPY

People give for all kinds of reasons, from family tradition to a sense of obligation to a desire to act on passionately held beliefs. Most giving follows the patterns of traditional philanthropy, operating under the charity model. Charity functions quite effectively in responding to acute crisis needs—blankets and food for flood victims, temporary housing for homeless families. The ability to respond to crises is one of traditional philanthropy's strongest assets. Traditional philanthropy is also very good at supporting the mainstream institutions—educational, research, religious, social and cultural—that are invested in maintaining and improving society and its structures. Traditional philanthropy is based on responding to, treating and managing the consequences of life in a society with a capital-based economy.

Progressive philanthropy, on the other hand, analyzes and responds more to cause than effect. Progressive philan-

thropy supports what is called social change, that is, actions that seek to right the imbalances of an unjust society or an unequal distribution of resources. For example, once warm and dry, flood victims may want to join together to advocate for effective yet environmentally sound flood control methods, including relocating businesses and houses out of the flood zone. To help homeless people, supporting a sweat-equity program and private-public partnerships for job training and education might provide more permanent solutions to their needs than funding shelters and food kitchens.

Progressive philanthropy strives to fund work that is proactive rather than reactive. Progressive philanthropy's investment lies in supporting and facilitating change, challenging the assumptions that economic and social inequities are somehow unavoidable as the price of progress or prosperity.

## CHANGING THE FACE OF PHILANTHROPY

Social change giving has taken on some new dimensions during the last 25 years. The social and economic justice movements of the 1960s—the Civil Rights Movement, the Student Movement and the Women's Movement—all appealed to the American beliefs in justice and equality for all, and thus encouraged many people to become active in working for social and economic change. At the same time, many young people who inherited wealth were not philosophically comfortable with automatically continuing the giving traditions of their parents and grandparents to the usual philanthropic recipients—hospitals, cultural institutions like opera and ballet, United Way and the Red Cross. Instead, they wanted to develop alternative avenues for funding that would support groups seeking the more fundamental social change represented by the social justice activities of their time.

Acting on these values, these young wealthy people joined with fellow activists of all income levels to create a number of public foundations across the country dedicated to addressing some of the root causes of inequity, including exploitation, racism, sexism and homophobia, and to broadening the traditional view of who gives to support fairness in America.

These foundations have catalysed a movement that sees people of all income levels as donors in support of change. Among other things, these foundations fund community organizing activities and sponsor alternative cultural institutions, including street theater, neighborhood arts and activist media. These foundations and others were catalysts in building the progressive funding movement, including networks such as the Funding Exchange, the National Network of Grantmakers and the Women's Funding Network.

The tremendous growth in the economy during the 1980s, especially in the world of technology, boosted many people's incomes through their work. Unlike old-money inheritors who came from a tradition of established philanthropy, these new millionaires are seeking their own ways to do useful and meaningful things with their money.

And millionaires are only a small proportion of those giving money away. In fact, an astounding 83 percent of the money donated in the United States each year comes from households with incomes of less than $60,000 a year.

That's good news because the federal government has rescinded much of its support for social services and corporate giving has barely grown. As a result of these cutbacks, responsibility for meeting some of the most basic needs of the poor and for responding to other social service, environmental and social justice needs has shifted onto the small base of nonprofit organizations. And these organizations need thoughtful, creative and effective giving now more than ever.

Chances are you give some amount of money away. Whether your giving is substantial enough to require itemization on your tax form or hovers around a thousand dollars a year, it is important that each dollar given and each hour spent have the greatest impact. Whether to give to the traditional recipients of philanthropy or to activities fostering social change is your choice. In either case, by following the thoughtful planning steps presented in this book, you'll succeed in maximizing the benefits of your gifts.

## CREATING A GIVING PLAN

*Inspired Philanthropy* will lead you through the steps to align your giving with your dreams of a better world. Creating and using a giving plan will give you a sense of control, purpose and direction, and will inspire you to become more pro-active in organizing, managing and taking charge of your financial life in general. A thoughtfully developed and conscientiously implemented giving plan will tell you where your philanthropic hours and dollars are going; and, because it reflects your personal priorities and dreams for creating a better world, it will be an active ally in supporting the issues that are most important to you.

Our world is growing more complex; environmental degradation, world strife and enormous social needs make thoughtful attention an ever more pressing demand. The good news is that there are more possibilities and tools for addressing these issues. As a donor, you can choose to utilize the tremendous opportunities for collaborating with those who share your vision, for seeding new ventures, for breaking down racial and socioeconomic barriers. As a person who cares about what happens in this world, your effectiveness, creativity, leadership and hope are needed as never before.

We offer *Inspired Philanthropy: Creating a Giving Plan* in a shared spirit of partnership for much-needed societal change.

## HOW TO USE THIS BOOK

Use the exercises and examples in *Inspired Philanthropy* to guide you through the process of developing your own personal giving plan, complete with mission statement, timeline and evaluation tools.

Included are worksheets that will lead you to articulate your priorities and values, inspiring stories of donors and nonprofit groups, and creative ideas for giving. We include up-to-date statistics on philanthropic giving, creative ideas for leveraging your dollars and time, sample language for making gifts such as bequests, and suggestions for additional reading and resource groups. We also include a discussion of how to say "no" graciously when family and friends knock on your door, along with sample letters of how to withdraw support from long-standing financial commitments.

We recommend that you read the entire book through once then go back through it more slowly, taking the time to do the exercises, write your mission statement and complete your giving plan. Start a folder or binder to hold your exercises, drafts of your mission statement and other materials so you can refer to them easily.

You also might want to consider reading the workbook with a group of friends or family members and developing your individual plans together. Working with others will both broaden your perspective and keep your momentum going toward becoming an inspired philanthropist.

## Some Beliefs about Inspired Philanthropy

- Everyone has a role in changing the inequities of society, regardless of income or class.
- Philanthropy is a creative expression of that part of yourself that cares about and believes in the potential for change.
- The most effective philanthropy joins your interests and experiences with the current needs in your community and seeks desired outcomes.
- Thoughtful, planned giving gives you a chance to express yourself and your passion as well as your goals and reasons for giving.
- Creating a giving plan fosters more enjoyment, ingenuity and effectiveness in personal philanthropy than automatic, reactive giving.
- Coming into your own true place of giving is an evolving, definable and developmental process.
- Inspired philanthropy and service have transforming powers for all—givers and receivers.

ONE

# Giving and the Nonprofit World

## Becoming an Inspired Philanthropist

**TRACEY MINKIN**

Our early giving was to the Sierra Club because my husband was a member and every time they called we'd give $25 or $35, but we had no idea how much we were giving over a year's time. One day I came across a brochure about giving that said that the people who earn the least give the most and that everyone should give 5 percent of their income. I went right home and suggested to Jonathan that we begin doing that.

The following year we made a list of our donations and noticed that, aside from gifts to our colleges, almost all our giving went to environmental groups. Although we were interested in social services, the environmental groups were the ones that had reached us. So we earmarked $2,000 (5 percent of our gross income of $40,000) and created categories of where we wanted to make donations: education, arts, social services and a slush fund.

As our income has risen so has our giving. We still divide it according to percentages we agree on and among groups we research. And the slush fund serves for whatever comes up—friends who ask us to buy tickets for things, for example. Our donations range from $25 to $1,500.

Each January we have what we call the Budget Summit. We used to have a bottle of champagne and have a party— that was before we had kids. We review our previous year's

giving and look at the groups in the slush fund to decide whether to include them in one of the other categories. We look at whether there will be anything big this year. For example, Jonathan wanted to give $1,000 to his 20th college reunion; next year he'll probably only give $250 and that will free up $750.

We keep track of our giving on a spreadsheet on the computer; with a few years all on one sheet, we can compare giving from previous years. We project how much the 5 percent is going to be and we go down the list to see what we did last year. We ask ourselves if we like the mix of groups. We talk substantially about how much to give to each group, trying to be realistic about the impact of the money. For example, $100 goes further at the local shelter than at a national environmental group like The Nature Conservancy, so we give a little more to The Nature Conservancy because we feel they're spending our money well. We're also interested in making a difference in our town, so we look for local opportunities to give.

We look at annual reports when they come, but not very closely. Instead, before the Budget Summit we have a lot of conversations on the fly about what we call good works. We've decided to put human or social services over other concerns, especially work for the well-being of children, and we value local over national or international efforts. We list all

5

the groups we want to give to for the next year and that's it.

When we get solicitations on the phone I ask them to send information or, if they are on our list, I ask them to send a pledge card that I will use when I've reviewed all my information. It makes it easy to always have the same answer.

When fundraising letters come from the groups on our list I write a check and note it on the spreadsheet. The major national environmental groups and schools do a good job of finding us and asking for money. Some groups who are on our list never ask us. In December, I write checks to groups that haven't asked. If something comes up during the year, for example, if I see an ad for the Women's Center and it looks like they need the money right now, I'll send them a check.

Sometimes you have to swallow hard to do this. We made less money this year so it's tempting to say, we could use this money this year. But we so firmly believe in philanthropy that we rely on our plan to keep us committed to our program—giving should be that way. We don't go to church and tithe regularly; for those of us who don't have that kind of system in place, it's too easy just not to do it.

I think people should start giving in their 20s, when they have a lot of energy and optimism and creativity, so they create an obligation towards it. It's also a time when you can get cynical if you're working at some low-paying job. Giving some money or volunteering is a great way to reaffirm your faith in the world and connect to something.

## MIVEN BOOTH TRAGESER

I created my first giving plan in the process of writing my will. I decided that I wanted 60 percent of my assets to go to specific nonprofit organizations and 40 percent to specific individuals.

In order to decide which organizations to include, I looked at the checks I had written as donations over the previous two years. There were certain themes: women's rights,

activism and social change, and media reform. I decided that each of these three areas would receive one-third of the 60 percent; I designated ten organizations within those areas and the proportion I wanted each of them to receive. When it came to naming individuals, ten people came to mind to whom $100 to $1,000 would make a difference and I named them in the will.

Making this plan forced me to realize that I can't give to everything. I had to confront that feeling of not being able to do enough for the world, that I have limitations.

At that point it became obvious to me that if I'm planning my giving for when I'm dead, why am I not doing it now? And I decided to take advantage of the work I had done on my will.

Then, after a couple of years of trying to give according to the plan, but not doing it, I looked over what I had been doing. I discovered that there were three organizations to which I'd given more than $250 each year for several years—Liberty Hill Foundation, the Labor Community Strategy Center and Co-op America. It felt good to realize that these were three organizations I had a good relationship with and felt good giving to each year, and that I could simplify my giving plan by focusing on them, as they support a range of activities I care about.

I know that there are lots of organizations I'm ignoring. I can't even let myself read their literature because I feel too upset that I'm not going to give them anything, because I'm committed to my plan. At the same time, there is something nice about saying no—I'm not going to spread myself any thinner. I have personal relationships with one or more people at all these organizations and I see them once a year or so.

I have never had a year where I followed my plan exactly the way I thought I would. I still find myself giving $30 to random phone solicitations or $10 at the front door. I thought the plan would arm me against that, because I would know I was being strategic. But I have a very hard time saying no to a kid at the front door.

## Nonprofits: An Essential Link

Nonprofit organizations are the most common vehicle for funneling money and other resources to areas of need. Nonprofits provide services, education and advocacy in a multitude of areas—from arts and culture, education, health, and public safety, to religion, recreation and community organizing. If you've ever checked out a library book, made a donation to the American Cancer Society, contributed to your church or school, volunteered as a monitor for a gay pride parade, donated your used clothing to a battered women's shelter, bought Girl Scout cookies, attended the ballet, symphony or opera, taken an aerobics class at your local YWCA or been a member of the Lions Club, you've been a citizen of the nonprofit world.

What is a nonprofit organization? Nonprofits, sometimes collectively referred to as the independent sector, are legally incorporated organizations defined under section 501(c)(3) of the Federal Tax Code as exempt from corporate income taxes because of their mission to accomplish some charitable, humanitarian or educational purpose. No owner, trustee or stockholder shares in any profits or losses of nonprofits.

A statistical view shows the enormous contribution of the independent sector to the country's economy. According to the 1996-1997 edition of the *Nonprofit Almanac*, in 1992 there were more than one million nonprofit institutions in the country, including schools, hospitals, human service agencies, arts and cultural organizations, churches, synagogues, temples and mosques. In 1994, the independent sector employed more than 15 million people (including the time donated by 93 million volunteers; with each contributing an average of 4.2 hours per week, they were considered the equivalent of five and one-half million full-time employees).

## How Nonprofits Affect Our Lives

What if there were no nonprofit organizations? Imagine…
- No community theaters, symphonies or museums
- No zoos, community gardens or farmers markets
- A rape victim without counseling and legal defense
- A town without a volunteer fire department, local Girl and Boy Scout chapters
- A rural community without a health clinic
- No AIDS or cancer research
- Injured or lost animals without humane rescue teams
- Lesbian, gay and questioning youth without welcoming crisis phone lines
- Natural disasters without the Red Cross
- No homeless shelters or soup kitchens
- No local churches, temples, synagogues or mosques
- No low-cost tuition and financial aid at schools or colleges
- No groups fighting to protect our environment and endangered species
- No community organizations fighting for justice
- No food banks, Salvation Army or Goodwill

Nonprofit organizations express some of the most caring aspects of our humanity and our desires for equality and justice. More than we may realize, our world counts on volunteers and donors.

A recent article in *The Economist* noted that "the nonprofit part of the economy accounts for 8 percent of the gross national product, a figure that has more than doubled since 1960; and it employs nearly 10 percent of the American workforce—more than the federal and state governments combined."

It is clear from these facts that nonprofits of all types play a crucial role in the social, economic, religious, cultural and community aspects of our lives.

## THAT'S A LOT OF MONEY

According to *Giving USA*, the annual yearbook on American philanthropy, in 1997, donations of nongovernmental funds to nonprofits totaled $143.5 billion.

If you're like most people, you probably think that most of the funds that go to charitable causes come from corporations and foundations. You're in for a surprise. More than 85 percent of the money given away in 1997—and for many years before that—came from individual donors (including those whose giving came in the form of bequests, that is, gifts distributed after their death). Corporations contributed 5.7 percent of the total, and foundations 9.3 percent. This general pattern has held true for a number of years.

When most of us think of the philanthropy of individuals, we think of large gifts by very wealthy people to such nonprofit institutions as universities, hospitals, museums and other traditional arts organizations, including symphony orchestras and ballet and opera companies. And in 1997 Ted

Turner's $1 billion gift to the United Nations set a very generous standard.

But here's another surprise: the bulk of money going to nonprofits actually comes from households with incomes of less than $60,000. Looked at another way, contributing households with incomes of *less than $10,000* give away a little more than 4 percent of their income to charity, while those with incomes of $100,000 or more give less as a percentage of income—only about 3.4 percent. Contributing households with incomes between $40,000 and $50,000 give on average only 1.3 percent. In relation to income, then, our largest and most generous donors are those who are the poorest.

What does this mean to you? It means that whether you give a lot or a little, when you join the community of donors—to traditional philanthropy or social change—you join millions of other Americans who make charitable gifts, and support nonprofit work that speaks to their ideas of caring and commitment to one another and the world.

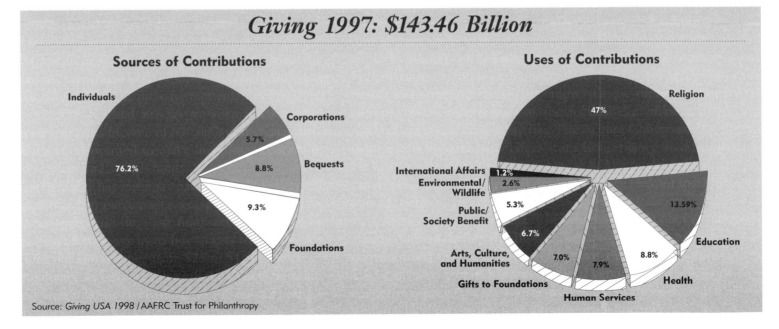

*Giving 1997: $143.46 Billion*

**Sources of Contributions**

Individuals 76.2%
Corporations 5.7%
Bequests 8.8%
Foundations 9.3%

**Uses of Contributions**

Religion 47%
Education 13.59%
Health 8.8%
Human Services 7.9%
Gifts to Foundations 7.0%
Arts, Culture, and Humanities 6.7%
Public/Society Benefit 5.3%
Environmental/Wildlife 2.6%
International Affairs 1.2%

Source: *Giving USA 1998* / AAFRC Trust for Philanthropy

## THE ROLE OF PRIVATE PHILANTHROPY

While private support of nonprofits rises a little each year, over the last few decades government support of nonprofits has been diminishing. As impossible as it is for private individuals to completely offset the government's extensive budget cuts to social services and arts institutions, the role of the individual donor is nevertheless increasing in importance as more and more nonprofits lose their governmental financial underpinnings.

At the same time the country's economy has been booming and, as the bar charts show, a small percentage of people at the top of the economic ladder have become much wealthier, while a growing number of people at the bottom have become poorer. For those who have benefited from the

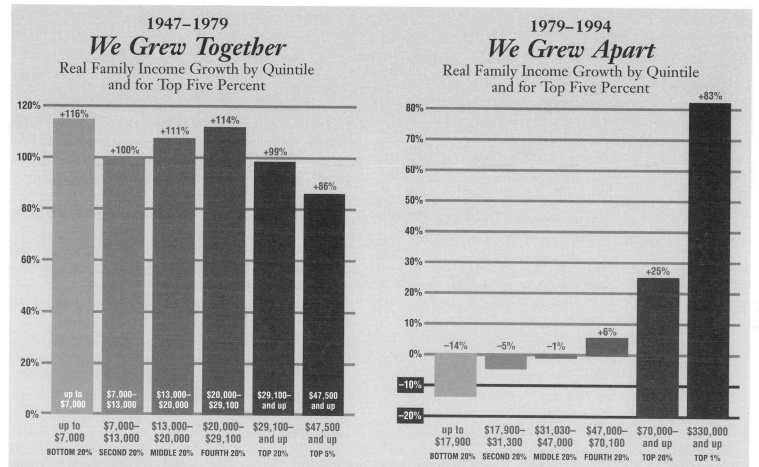

### 1947–1979
## *We Grew Together*
Real Family Income Growth by Quintile
and for Top Five Percent

| | +116% | +100% | +111% | +114% | +99% | +86% |
|---|---|---|---|---|---|---|
| | up to $7,000 | $7,000– $13,000 | $13,000– $20,000 | $20,000– $29,100 | $29,100 and up | $47,500 and up |
| | BOTTOM 20% | SECOND 20% | MIDDLE 20% | FOURTH 20% | TOP 20% | TOP 5% |

*Sources:* Analysis of Census Bureau data by Lawrence Mishel & Jared Berstein *The State of Working America 1994-95* p. 37 Income Ranges in 1979 dollars from March 1996 Census Current Population Survey, Table H-1

### 1979–1994
## *We Grew Apart*
Real Family Income Growth by Quintile
and for Top Five Percent

| | –14% | –5% | –1% | +6% | +25% | +83% |
|---|---|---|---|---|---|---|
| | up to $17,900 | $17,900– $31,300 | $31,030– $47,000 | $47,000– $70,100 | $70,000 and up | $330,000 and up |
| | BOTTOM 20% | SECOND 20% | MIDDLE 20% | FOURTH 20% | TOP 20% | TOP 1% |

*Sources:* March 1996 Census Current Population Survey, Table F-1 and F-1a.
Top 1% Income in 1993 dollars: CBO data cited by Paul Krugman, *Peddling Prosperity,* p. 135

Charts courtesy of United for a Fair Economy

## What's Underfunded

- Groups serving women and girls
- International groups
- Environmental groups
- Groups serving people of color
- Groups led by people of color
- Groups serving lesbians and gays
- Community-based arts programs
- Rurally based programs
- Programs for refugees and immigrants
- Bilingual programs
- Alternative health care programs
- Mental health services for low-income clients
- Programs for single parents and their families
- Low-income housing
- Systemic change programs and strategies
- Policy and research
- Collaborations, especially statewide
- Media and access to media and technology
- General operating support (instead of project-specific funds)

good economic times, investments in a long-bullish stock market have made them even wealthier.

Inspired philanthropy poses these questions: Given the currently low levels of government funding for social services and other nonprofit activity, what is the responsibility of each of us? And do those with higher incomes or more assets have a greater responsibility? We believe that we all have a responsibility as citizens of the human community to give as much of ourselves as we can. For those of us whose personal wealth or earnings have grown, we feel we should consider matching our expanded financial resources and options with equally strong community generosity.

## What Motivates People to Give

What is the inspiration that motivates people to give? The answer is, of course, somewhat different for everyone. Some of us follow the tradition and examples of giving and volunteering we were raised with. Others are moved by witnessing injustice. What is almost indisputable is that in the act of giving time, skills or money, we feel the spark of our original inspiration, which propels us to continue giving.

The following are inspirational stories of donors with unique motivations and passions for giving and an organized, focused vision that has developed over time.

### SARAH SILBER: Growing Up Giving

From the time she was born, Sarah Silber received small gifts of money on her birthday and at Hanukkah. When she was nine, her parents deposited this money in a special "gift" account for Sarah, and showed her the meaning of the account's interest and balance figures. When Sarah was 16, her grandmother encouraged her to begin contributing some of her savings (then $3,200) and her time to projects that interested her. Grandmother and granddaughter made a deal: for every hour Sarah volunteered and for every dollar she gave of her own money, her grandmother would contribute a dollar to Sarah's "Giving Fund" for future use.

Sarah began keeping newspaper and magazine articles, brochures and flyers about issues and groups that interested her. After a while she noticed that most of the information she had collected was about dolphins and abused children. She realized that one way she could do something to help in these areas was to give money to the projects that excited her.

To help her decide which groups could use her donations the most, Sarah made a list based on her collection of materials, and took it to the library. There she found that three of the organizations on her list that work to rehabilitate injured dolphins were mentioned in a book on national environmental nonprofits. She also learned about the Environmental Support Center in Washington, D.C., which she wrote to for more ideas. With all this information, she began making some donations.

Now 23, Sarah gets a sense of the groups she supports through reading their mailings or visiting the projects themselves. She keeps files alphabetically by organization, and for each file she has created a contact sheet to remind her of her past ideas and actions with the groups. Her donations to the organizations are sometimes in her name and sometimes in honor of friends or other family members. Since she turned 18, Sarah has been giving away $300 a year.

At first Sarah resisted creating a giving plan. But she now routinely picks up material about groups that might interest her and puts them in her files. She has developed her own funding cycle, writing checks only twice a year: around the time of her birthday and the year-end holidays.

Since she collects and files information all year, Sarah spends only about 20 minutes at the end of each year creating her plan. She reports that it helps her stay focused and keep her priorities clear, and it makes it easier to turn down requests for donations outside of her giving categories or funding cycles.

## PETER AND JONATHAN: A Couple's Commitment

Peter and Jonathan are both committed environmentalists and give regularly to nonprofits, sometimes in cash, sometimes in securities they own. When they read that the Women's Forest Sanctuary was looking for investors to help refinance mortgages on 14 acres of old-growth redwoods, they decided they would like to help. They sold some of their stock and loaned the money to the Forest Sanctuary for a modest 6 percent return.

Though this meant a lower return than they had been making in the stock market, the decision gratified them. As Jonathan said, "It gave us the chance to feel part of saving one of the world's greatest resources. Given that we're only in our 30s, have good earning potential, and don't need to use income from our stocks now, this was an easy decision—but our love of the trees was the highest value."

As a side benefit, they avoid the higher capital gains taxes they were previously paying on their high-earning stocks.

## GREG GARVAN: Giving Back

In the early 1990s, Greg Garvan received a modest inheritance, giving him many new choices. But Greg and his wife were hard-put to know how to handle these new choices. "Do we give all or part away, keep it for retirement, save some for the kids?" they asked themselves.

First they followed the age-old advice not to make any major changes for a year. During the year, they met with a financial planner to review their options. At the end of the year, they had made their decision: they would give 25 percent away outright and with the rest set up gifts to nonprofits through charitable annuities (see Chapter Ten) that would add to their retirement.

In thinking about the kinds of nonprofits he wanted to give to, Greg decided to support small groups that others might not be funding and that would have some personal meaning to him. Since his family had owned a textile company for 120 years in the South, the profits of which had contributed to his inheritance, Greg and his wife decided to give back to those people whose relatives had been underpaid by the textile business.

Through his own travel and research, Greg found small organizations—not funded by larger regional foundations—that help local minority farmers and new businesses. One was the South Carolina Farming Association's Seeds of Hope project, which links Black farmers with local churches to set up farmers' markets. The program had become so successful that churches far outside the local area wanted produce for their own farmers' markets. To be able to transport fresh produce to these more distant markets, the project needed a refrigeration truck. Learning of this need, Greg and his family provided the money to buy the truck.

In another philanthropic area, Greg convinced his siblings to join him in supporting the Black Historical Society and in honoring a Black woman who had helped raise them by establishing the Carrie Kilgore Scholarship at the College of Charleston. "This is a modest way of saying our thanks to someone who gave so much to each of us," says Greg.

Greg and his family also helped the Institute of Southern Studies, publishers of the magazine *Southern Exposure*, with a year's start-up funding to hire a marketing and fundraising specialist.

Greg's advice to donors is, "Talk to folks. Groups usually know what they need or want to try. Do you have the ability to respond to their request? Try to do some homework about the group's financial situation or vision, or check out their collaborations. Then say yea or nay. But have fun doing it! If you're lucky enough, a good part of your community nonprofit investments will work and be a spiritual experience. In the meantime, you'll also grow and learn so much about your community! What could be better!"

### JOHN GAGE: Living and Giving Simply

A former monk, 50-year-old John Gage left the Jesuit order ten years ago but still keeps his vow of simplicity. He feels strongly that America is caught up in over-consuming, and finds it troubling that most people do not see or feel the effects of what he considers to be global greed. Although he lives on less than $8,000 a year, John gives away $480 annually (6 percent of his income). He still focuses his giving on the goal of "restoring right relationship between peoples and the planet" that informed the giving practices of his Jesuit order. In choosing which nonprofit organizations to donate to, John creates a giving plan that includes:

- setting a budget
- establishing annual mission statements or "hopeful goals"
- sorting direct mail contribution requests regularly in order to help groups eliminate duplications and to keep informed through their updates
- supporting investigative reporting in order to learn more about who is working for social justice
- favoring low-profile groups that don't send elaborate or multiple mailings, and whose communications are environmentally sensitive
- initiating personal contact with at least half of the groups to which he gives in order to ask them what they need in terms of money or support.

## Finding Your Own Inspiration

In the following chapters, *Inspired Philanthropy* will take you step-by-step through the process of developing and implementing a Personal Giving Plan. With this guide, you'll examine your vision of a just and compassionate world, acquire the tools to search out those organizations that share your vision, evaluate their effectiveness, focus your philanthropic resources, exercise control over your own decisions, and experience a sense of satisfaction and joy from making a real contribution to a better future.

# TWO

# You, the Philanthropist

## Who Is a Philanthropist?

Probably very few people write "philanthropist" as their profession on their income tax returns. For most of us, philanthropy is not our occupation—it is an offshoot of whatever we do with the rest of our time. Even if philanthropy occupies a larger share of one's time, to think of it as a title can seem daunting, raising a multitude of negative stereotypes and assumptions.

What images or feelings come to mind when you think of the word philanthropist? We all carry stereotypes of philanthropists, though we may not be conscious of them most of the time. Allowing ourselves to recognize these stereotypes and then contrast them with our actual experience helps to free us from long-held biases. Check out your own ideas about philanthropy in Exercise 1.

---

**Exercise 1**        **STEREOTYPES**        10–20 minutes

Allow yourself to write whatever comes to your mind, uncensored. By getting at the ideas that are just below the surface we can begin to identify our stereotypes—and, if appropriate, discard them.

**Typical philanthropists:**
*(Example: Are from old money; are older than 55; live in mansions.)*

a. _____

b. _____

c. _____

**People I know who give are:**

a. _____

b. _____

c. _____

**As a giver I am:**

a. _____

b. _____

c. _____

**Reflection:** What have you learned about yourself in doing this exercise? For example, you may have found that your stereotypes contradict your experience or that the terms "philanthropist" and "giver" elicit different reactions.

_____

_____

_____

_____

Let's look at this notion of philanthropy a little more closely. The word philanthropy derives from Greek and literally means love of humankind. According to the *Oxford English Dictionary*, a philanthropist is "one who from love of his fellow men exerts himself for their well-being; engages in practical benevolence towards men in general." Inspired philanthropy expands that description to define as philanthropists "all people who exert themselves for the well-being of others; who engage in practical and heartfelt benevolence; who donate money and time to causes they believe in so that the world may become a better place."

If you've given away money (or volunteered time) you're a philanthropist, whether you donate millions to a new hospital wing, a few hundred dollars to a community health clinic or $25 to a nursery school raffle. The money can come from earned income, inherited wealth or a windfall at a bingo game. The two essential ingredients are giving and caring. When you give to those things you care deeply about, your philanthropy develops special meaning.

The fact is there is no threshold of activity or money one must achieve to qualify as a philanthropist. Philanthropy is the design and manifestation of your hopes, dreams and wishes. If you don't do so already, calling any donations of time or money your "philanthropy" will give it the intention it deserves. You give because you care about others.

Creating a giving plan is a process of distilling what you love and are concerned with, and threading those issues with your own values, money and time; it's also choosing initiatives, leaders and nonprofits whose missions and strategies are working to make the changes you want to see.

# What Do You Care About?

*Giving well requires that I listen to my inner self and make more conscious who I am and what I want to express in the world. That's why giving is almost always satisfying to me—whether or not the projects I fund are successful.*

—HARRIET BARLOW

Knowing what you feel passionate about is the first step in determining how your personal contributions of money, time and energy will be most effective. Your financial resources are part of who you are. Giving money is about giving a part of yourself.

The next exercises ask you to look at what you value most and whether your funding choices to this point reflect those values. For many philanthropists, giving is not only a way to express their values, it also helps them articulate what they are.

Our values are characteristics we hold in high esteem, things we give worth to. We may value qualities of being, such as integrity and justice, or particular kinds of endeavors, such as working for justice for the oppressed, feeding those who are hungry, or elevating the status of women. Whether we are conscious of them, our values greatly influence our behavior as givers, including what we fund, how we evaluate projects, and how we relate to those we support. For example, if you value women's leadership, you may make it a priority to fund programs that give women opportunities to develop leadership skills. Even if a program you're interested in is not specially oriented to women, you may want to know what percentage of their members and key staff are women. If you're considering a larger gift, you may request to meet with women in leadership in the group.

Exercises 2 and 3 can help you clarify your values as a giver.

# INDICATORS OF YOUR VALUES

In whatever way works best for you—free writing, quiet thought, or a conversation with a friend—explore one or more of the following questions that you find interesting. Write your answers below.

- What experiences and people have been key in shaping your core values and passions?

_____

_____

_____

_____

_____

- What do you notice about your values when you consider your choices, such as life directions, career, free time, lifestyle, donations and spending?

_____

_____

_____

_____

_____

- When you hear of world events or witness an injustice, what moves you most? With what have you been most troubled? Most delighted?

_____

_____

_____

_____

_____

# IT'S IN THE CARDS

*At the back of the book you'll find two sheets of preprinted and blank cards. Cut them out. On one sheet are words or phrases that express values. (They are also listed on the following page.) Feel free to add any that are especially meaningful to you on the cards left blank.*

Choose from the deck your top five values. Even though it may be difficult, out of those five cards choose your top three and record them here.

**Top three values:**

1. _____

2. _____

3. _____

*On the second set of cards (and also on the next page) are words or phrases that describe issue areas and populations that you may care about as a contributor. The areas provided are only for inspiration. You may never have donated time or money to these areas of interest before; this exercise is simply to give you the chance to recognize what has meaning for you among things you could give to.*

Choose from this deck your top five areas, then your top three. List these here. If one of the three is of absolutely the highest priority, star it.

**Top three interest areas and concerns:**

1. _____

2. _____

3. _____

**Reflection:**

Do you see a relationship between your top values and your top interest areas? Here are two examples:

*1. My top three values are dignity, equality and opportunity and my top three issue areas are education, economic justice and youth development. I believe that the opportunity for a good education, particularly for young people who are shut out of their full potential early on because of poor schools, is vital to dignity, equality and, finally, economic justice for everyone.*

*2. My top three values are community, justice and respect and my top three issue areas are seniors, poverty and homelessness/housing. The relationship I see is that in order for everyone to live in a just community, all seniors must have enough financial support, including good housing, to lead their lives with respect.*

Write down the relationships you see among your own values and interests:

_____

_____

_____

_____

_____

_____

_____

_____

_____

_____

_____

_____

# Values

| | | | |
|---|---|---|---|
| Acceptance | Dignity | Interdependence | Respect |
| Beauty | Diversity | Integrity | Responsibility |
| Commitment | Equality | Justice | Service |
| Communication | Faith | Joy | Simplicity |
| Community | Family | Knowledge | Transformation |
| Compassion | Freedom | Love | _____ |
| Courage | Harmony | Opportunity | |
| Creativity | Healing | Peace | _____ |
| Democracy | Honesty | Preservation | |
| | | | _____ |

# Issue Areas and Populations

| | | | |
|---|---|---|---|
| AIDS | Domestic Violence | Homelessness / Housing | Prison Reform |
| Animals | Economic Justice | Human Rights | Public Policy / Advocacy |
| Anti-Semitism | Education | Immigrant & Refugee Rights and Services | Reproductive Rights |
| Anti-Racism | Employment Training & Job Creation | International Development | Seniors |
| Arts & Art Institutions | Environment / Environmental Justice | Jewish Causes | Spiritual Development |
| Boys | | Legal Aid | Sports |
| Catholic Charities | Electoral Reform | Libraries | Sustainable Development |
| Children | Faith-Based Community Service | Media | Women's Rights |
| Civil Rights | Gay/Lesbian/ Bisexual Civil Rights | Native & Indigenous Peoples' Rights | Youth Development |
| Community Gardens | | Parks & Land Preservation | _____ |
| Corporate Responsibility | Girls | Peace / Conflict Resolution | |
| Demilitarization | Gun Control | Philanthropy & Volunteerism | _____ |
| Disability Rights | Healthcare & Medical Research | Poverty | |
| Disaster Relief | | | _____ |
| Drug & Alcohol Abuse | | | |

## What Do You Bring with You?

Working with organizations as a donor is, for many, an unexpected source of satisfaction. Experienced donors report that some of the benefits of their work as donor activists have been developing and sharing a wide variety of skills. Putting what you do well in the service of a cause you feel passionate about and being recognized for your contribution feels won-derful. In turn, you'll invariably learn more as a result of your philanthropy, which is also immensely rewarding.

In the last exercise, you explored what's important to you and what you believe in. Now it's time to give some thought to additional skills, knowledge, training and back-ground you have to offer. These may be personal experience with an issue area, specific expertise and knowledge, and/or skills and abilities you can put to use.

---

| Exercise 4 | TIME, TALENTS AND TREASURES | 15–25 minutes |
| --- | --- | --- |

What time, talents and treasures do you bring to your passion? In the list below put a check mark next to each characteristic or item you have. These may stimulate you to think of specific ways you want to share your abilities, which is the purpose of the second part of the exercise.

☐ I can donate my professional skills to a nonprofit

☐ My workplace has equipment or services I could offer to a nonprofit for their use

☐ I'm good at organizing details and creating plans

☐ I'm good at motivating people

☐ I'm good at planning events and giving parties

☐ I know many people in my community who might be good resources

☐ I like to teach what I know

☐ I am a good listener or writer

☐ I am a supportive person to work with

☐ I'm good with financial information

☐ I like to raise money

☐ I can translate documents into other languages

☐ I have graphic skills or artistic talents

☐ I am a passionate public speaker

☐ I have _____ hours of time per week to donate

☐ Other: _____

Now look back at the top three values and issue areas you wrote down on page 16. Based on the list at left, think about the time, talent and resources unique to you and your community that you can offer in work-ing on those issue areas. For example, if you're a breast cancer survivor and one of your issue areas is breast cancer, you might write, "I have been through diagnoses and treatment and could help others know what to expect or just provide support." Or, if you're passionate about elec-toral reform and belong to a civic group or business roundtable, you could invite a speaker on the topic to make a presentation.

Write a statement of how you can offer your time, talents and treasures here:

_____

_____

_____

_____

_____

_____

_____

_____

_____

# Your Current System of Giving

Everyone has a system of giving. It may be as unsophisticated as the time-honored shoe box—throw every direct mail piece into a box and once a month, once a year, pull them out and write checks for the ones that appeal to you. Or it may be more spontaneous—write a check whenever an appeal strikes you as worthwhile, or someone asks, or an event seems like it might be important or fun. Or it may be as formal as directing your broker to send a check each November 15 to the charity your family has been supporting for generations.

Taking the time to pull together what you've been doing and looking at it as a whole will tell you more about yourself than you realize. To develop intentionality and consciousness about how you give, to whom, how much, when and for how long, it helps to look at how you've been doing it up to now.

| Exercise 5 | ANALYSIS OF CURRENT GIVING | 15-20 minutes |
|---|---|---|

**A. Recent Giving** —To get a sense of where your giving has gone in the last year, fill out the chart below.

| ORGANIZATIONS DONATED TO IN THE LAST 12 MONTHS | AMOUNT GIVEN | WHY I GAVE |
|---|---|---|
| | | |
| | | |
| | | |
| | | |
| | | |
| | | |
| | | |
| | | |

*Continued on next page*

*Exercise 5 continued from previous page…*

## B. Characteristics of the Groups You Give To — Beginning with the list of organizations you generated, map your top ten groups on the chart below. (See the list of strategies groups may employ on the next page.) Once you've done so, you'll begin to see the patterns of your giving.

| ORGANIZATION | ISSUES IT ADDRESSES<br>refer to list on page 17 | STRATEGIES IT EMPLOYS<br>refer to next page | SIZE BY BUDGET<br>*small:* less than $250,000<br>*medium:* $250,000 +<br>*large:* more than $1million | AGE<br>*start up:* 0–2 years<br>*new:* 2–5 years<br>*established:* 5–10 years<br>*sustained:* 10 plus years | SCOPE<br>local, state/regional,<br>national, international |
|---|---|---|---|---|---|
|  |  |  |  |  |  |
|  |  |  |  |  |  |
|  |  |  |  |  |  |
|  |  |  |  |  |  |
|  |  |  |  |  |  |
|  |  |  |  |  |  |
|  |  |  |  |  |  |
|  |  |  |  |  |  |

**Reflection:**

1. Within each set of characteristics, was your giving focused around certain categories, or varied? Were these intentional choices? If they were, what reasons were behind your choices?

_____

_____

2. What do you see as the pros and cons of the pattern your giving has taken within each category? (For instance, your dollars may have greater impact on smaller, start-up organizations, but start-ups sometimes fail. Giving locally offers you more personal connection, yet many serious problems are international in scope, and your dollar often goes further overseas.)

_____

_____

3. Based on the characteristics of the groups you've funded, is there anything you would like to do differently next year? What? Why?

_____

_____

*Continued on next page*

*Exercise 5 continued from previous page…*

## C. Your Relationship with Groups You Gave To

Look again at the groups you listed in Section B of this exercise, and take stock of the relationships you have with them below:

**1. With what number of organizations are you a:**
_____ Recipient of the organization's services
_____ Volunteer
_____ Member
_____ Board member
_____ Staff member
_____ Other: _____

**2. With how many do you:**
_____ Know people in the organization
_____ Know people who have been affected or helped personally by the organization (or ones like it)
_____ Know other donors

**3. With how many did you find out about them through:**
_____ Direct mail
_____ Family, friends or work colleagues
_____ Local public foundation
_____ Media
_____ Other: _____

**4. With how many do you:**
_____ Want your donation to be completely anonymous
_____ Want your donation held in confidence (only one or two people in the recipient organization know)
_____ Don't care whether your donation is known
_____ Want people in the community to know you made a donation

**5. With how many did you stay informed by:**
_____ Reading newsletters or annual reports
_____ Attending events
_____ Meeting one-on-one with staff or board
_____ Other: _____

**Reflection:**

1. Are your connections with the groups you gave to close or distant? Has this been an intentional choice?

_____
_____

2. Do you see pros and cons of giving where you have relationships, and building relationships where you give? For instance, if you have no personal relationship to groups you fund, your giving may feel too abstract to be compelling. On the other hand, by supporting only groups with which you have close ties you may miss out on supporting other worthwhile organizations.

_____
_____

3. How have you felt about your previous giving? Based on your relationship to the groups you've given to, is there anything you would do differently next year? Why?

_____
_____

# Strategies for Change

- Advocacy
- Public Interest Law
- Coalition Building
- Demonstrating or Public Education

- Economic Development
- Education, Training and Resource Development
- Funding Infrastructure (core operating expenses)

- Electoral Politics (supporting candidates and initiatives; voter education and registration)
- Grassroots Community Organizing
- Human or Direct Services

- Influencing Public Policy
- Prayer, Meditation and Reflection-based Action
- Problem Analysis and Research

# Imagining a Better World

The information you generated in the last exercise describes your present giving practices and something about how you operate as a giver. When looked at as a whole in this way, your giving choices may surprise you—both in clarifying where your priorities are and in what characterizes the groups you gave to. The strategy, size, age and scope of those groups reflect how they make an impact. Maybe it's time to take a new look at where you want to be part of creating change.

The next two exercises offer you the chance to step back from the giving you've been doing and reflect on social change in a broader sense. What are the reasons behind some of the problems that concern you? What do you wish were different, and what might help change the situation? Realistic answers to these questions are usually frighteningly complex, yet it is worth trying to articulate answers, even at the risk of oversimplifying, because you will learn a lot about what you want to be giving to. If Exercise 6 seems daunting to you at first, you might want to skip to Exercise 7 for another way of getting at your vision of what you might create. Whichever exercise you choose, keep in mind that, like most of the exercises in this book, this is not one you can do once and learn all you need to know. In fact, it may open a dialogue with yourself and others about why change is needed on issues you care deeply about, what changes could be most useful, and how you can contribute.

---

| Exercise 6 | IMAGINING A BETTER WORLD | Part 1: 30 minutes / Part 2: 30 minutes |

This exercise is in two parts, one cerebral, the other imaginative. The first part asks you and a supportive, interested friend or friends to think deeply about an issue, how things came to be the way they are and what might help create positive change. The second part calls on your imagination to move beyond the rational thought process to an imagined state of an improved world. The two parts do not have to be done together. An example of doing this exercise using the topic of homelessness is on the next page.

Choose one topic that is of significant concern to you—something you'd really like to have an effect on in the world. (If you're having trouble defining a topic, refer to the list on page 17.)

.........................................................................................................

## PART 1: How did things get the way they are? What might help them to change?

With your friend who shares your interest or concern, brainstorm what you know about this issue and present some of your main questions. You may want to consider key historical events, public education and opinion, and interests of proponents and opponents of various actions to address the issue. This part of the exercise may lead you to do some research to inform yourself more fully about the issue. When you've completed your thinking, list some of the ways the issue has been dealt with in the past and possible ways to change it in the future. On the next page is an example using the topic of homelessness.

## PART 2: Imagining a better world

In some quiet time alone, or with your companion of Part 1, project your imagination into a world in which the issue you discussed in Part 1 has been positively changed 100 percent. For example, imagine an end to discrimination, or all endangered species flourishing. Daydream about the specific circumstances that would be different in this new world.

When you're finished, reflect on your vision the way you would if you were thinking about a dream you had just woken from. Choose one piece that strikes you. Look for what is most exciting, intriguing or surprising in your vision, something you would love to see in your eyes-open, real-life world. Brainstorm with yourself or your friend ways this piece could inspire a new area to fund or a new approach to your giving.

*Continued on next page*

## AN EXAMPLE OF IMAGINING A BETTER WORLD
# TOPIC: HOMELESSNESS

**PART 1: Why is there homelessness in the United States? What might help this to change?**

**Key historical events, public opinion & interests:**

- Federal policies in the early 1980s sent a majority of patients in state institutions to the streets, and failed to provide the community services promised to help them
- Other federal cutbacks in the 1980s severely reduced funding for subsidized housing
- "Panhandler" laws prohibiting homeless people from asking for money have passed in many cities
- Widespread corporate downsizing and relocation to other countries in the 1980s and 1990s left many low-level workers without jobs
- Today, after many years of widespread, visible homelessness, the general public has become hardened to it and concerned about their own safety
- Many city governments seem concerned more about keeping homeless people out of downtown areas where they disrupt commerce than with trying to meet their needs for food and shelter

**Questions:**

- What is forcing people to become homeless right now?
- What are the characteristics of different populations of homeless people (women with children, substance abusers, etc.)?
- What are the specific needs in my city? For example, are there enough shelters? Do they stay open year-round?
- What helps people to find homes and jobs again?

**Possible actions and keys to change:**

- Pressuring politicians to enact proactive and humane policies
- Job training for available jobs and subsidized housing programs
- Public education that emphasizes how close many families are to homelessness
- Government assistance systems that provide minimum financial security, basic health care and mental health services
- Working for "living wage" campaigns, greater access to affordable housing and small business loans and tax reform—all of which would move us toward a more equitable distribution of wealth

**PART 2: Imagining an end to homelessness**

In your vision, our culture would place a high value on everyone's quality of life. Nonprofit organizations, religious institutions and city governments would support the infrastructure that provides services such as job training, career counseling and apprenticeships. There would be enough safe, clean shelters for people who needed them, including adequate facilities for women with children. People who lost their jobs or for some other reason, such as family illness, suddenly had their income threatened, would have access to friendly and forthcoming government welfare programs, including housing, food and transportation vouchers, and health care.

One piece that might strike you most could be job training and career counseling programs that would be open to anyone who needed them. You could begin by phoning your local church, synagogue or shelter to find out what programs exist and what they need most. They may need volunteers to go through the newspaper's classified section with job seekers and phone employers on their behalf, or they may need interview clothes and voicemail for people looking for jobs, or bus and taxi vouchers for people going to interviews. You might see a way that you personally could begin to make a difference in the lives of some of the homeless people in your area.

## PULLING IT ALL TOGETHER

Here's your chance to play Monopoly. But instead of hoarding your money and buying up all the properties, use the next exercise to create your vision of how you would give it away.

---

| Exercise 7 | MILLION DOLLAR VISIONING | 30–45 minutes |

1. From the list of values and issues you care about, think of a problem in society you would really like to help resolve:

_____

_____

_____

2. Now, imagine you have just been given $1,000,000 to give away or invest in solving that problem, with no strings attached. What would you do, who would you convene or hire to support your efforts, what institutional partners would you choose?

_____

_____

_____

3. What outcomes would you hope for in what time frame?

_____

_____

_____

4. How would you be involved to maximize impact?

_____

_____

_____

5. How would you share your vision with others?

_____

_____

_____

6. What is holding you back from starting some of this work, even without $1,000,000 currently before you?

_____

_____

_____

# Learning More about Social Change

The previous exercises may have stimulated you to want to know more about what really causes things to change. How do trends shift away from harmful practices and toward more constructive behaviors? There are many resources for informing your thinking about social change, both general theory about how change happens and studies of specific issue areas.

In the next week, give yourself some time to look into how you might learn about social change. For example, go to a library or bookstore and see what books there are on the topic; look into a class at an adult education center or local community college; interview one or more people who have been effective at making change in an area you care about; watch a video or film on the topic; talk to others who have focused on an area that also concerns you.

If, for example, a factory in your town moved its work to another country in order to pay their workers lower wages, you might want to get involved in some action. How do you begin? You could start at the library or bookstore with books on economic globalization. Your research might lead you to some nonprofits working on the issue, including the Institute for Policy Studies' Globalization Project. Or you could consider taking a class on the topic, or attend a local meeting with displaced workers, or find others who have focused on the issue.

When you've laid out some options, choose one or two of them and schedule time to do them in the next month or two.

Increasing your knowledge base and experience will greatly increase your effectiveness as a citizen and a donor, and continue to help you refine your own philanthropic mission. The next chapter brings together what you've learned about yourself and giving so far and brings you to the first step of creating your giving plan: your philanthropic mission statement.

# FOUR

# Creating a Mission Statement

In the last chapters you looked at your stereotypes about what a philanthropist is, who you are in terms of your values, interests and priorities, what skills you bring to the nonprofit world, where you've invested charitable donations in the past, and how you think the issues you care most deeply about might be changed for the better.

You've done a lot of thinking and learned a lot about yourself. All of this information will be useful in the next step: creating a philanthropic mission statement.

Your mission statement is a short description that answers the question, "What do I want to do with my giving and my time and why?" Once created and refined to your satisfaction, your mission statement will guide you in developing your Inspired Philanthropy Giving Plan in Chapter Seven. If your family is giving together, now is the time to articulate a collective vision.

## Writing Your Mission Statement

The most effective mission statements are usually no more than two or three sentences—something you can easily remember and others can easily understand. Though a mission statement is brief, it needs to pack a lot of information in it, so it will take some work to get it to say just what you want.

To begin, review your top values and interests from Exercise 3 on page 16. Next, revisit what you felt you could offer of your time, talents and treasures in Exercise 4. And, finally, look at where you imagined you might like to make some significant changes in the world in Exercises 6 and/or 7. With this information, you're ready to try your hand at drafting a mission statement. Here are some mission statements that others have written.

### SOME INSPIRED MISSION STATEMENTS FROM INDIVIDUALS AND FAMILY FOUNDATIONS

I seek to reduce the amount of violence within families in my community. I do this by supporting family violence prevention programs, volunteering 10 hours a month on parent telephone hotlines to reduce stress in families, continuing my 10-year commitment as a Big Brother, and advocating for laws that punish crimes of violence against families and that protect victims of violence.

• • •

I want to see social justice, economic redistribution and racial harmony. Therefore, I work for, donate to and volunteer with organizations that involve ordinary people in confronting and changing the institutions and public policies that affect their lives. I especially like to support those organizations in which I am personally involved, or where I know leaders of the organization.

The Compassionate Soul Fund exists to model gift giving and to raise consciousness about women's multiple contributions to the world. We fund feminist projects for social change and human rights, especially those that serve and are headed by indigenous women and women of color.

• • •

The Seed Fund exists to provide seeds to low-income communities for gardening and soup kitchens. We are a group of organic farmers who believe that healthy food and hands-on growing and cooking of food can change the health and well-being of any community. We make contributions of money and/or seeds to schools and projects that distribute seeds, and we establish community gardens and teach sustainable gardening.

• • •

I've seen children gain enormous self-confidence, skills and new friends through camp experiences that have helped transform their lives. I believe that camp should be an experience available to all kids. Our family has established the Campers Fund to give scholarships to low-income and disabled children who have never been to camp before. It is our family goal to help 2–4 kids per year with $500 to $750 each for scholarships to the summer camp of their choosing.

• • •

I believe that people meeting people in beautiful settings and sharing consciousness can catalyze change. I seek to give opportunity for those who have little access to changemakers to meet them. I do this through sending people to conferences so they may meet other leaders, through the creation of a writers' retreat so they may have more time for reflection, and through connecting people through contacts I have. I commit to give one-fourth of my income to this effort annually, and to volunteer two hours each week toward this work.

• • •

I am deeply concerned about the effects of industrial pollution on the environment. I believe that grassroots action by communities to oppose pollution in their neighborhoods is one effective way to address this issue. Therefore, I donate to nonprofit groups that confront this issue on a local scale.

• • •

I want to help immigrants to this country. Everyone in my family from my grandparents' generation were immigrants and the country has been good for us. I fund groups that give immediate support to immigrants and help them obtain good free or low-cost legal aid.

• • •

As a lifelong student, I know the value of a good education. I devote whatever extra money and time I have to helping students who might otherwise never get formal educational opportunities.

• • •

My personal mission is to change the world (including the world of philanthropy) so that real equity exists in all places for all people. I do this through supporting diversity in the organizations I support with my donations and time and through donating to political candidates who represent minority constituents.

• • •

Our family's goal is to bring creative expression to our community. We fund art and photography classes for inner-city and rural young people, ages 12–18, and have established a summer community arts program that works with more than 200 young people each summer in our town. In addition, we buy art from emerging artists for personal investment and joy.

# YOUR MISSION STATEMENT

Write your own philanthropic mission statement here. It should include: 1. Reference to your passionate interests; 2. What you think can help improve/change issues you care most about; 3. What you are doing to support improvement/change. We've provided room for a couple of first drafts.

First Draft:

_____

_____

_____

_____

_____

_____

_____

Second Draft:

_____

_____

_____

_____

_____

_____

Final Statement:

_____

_____

_____

_____

_____

_____

_____

# FIVE

# How Much Do You Want to Give?

As an individual donor, your contributions will fall into two categories: money and time. These, in turn, encompass a variety of options. In the money category, you may want to donate smaller amounts to several organizations and larger amounts to one, or a few. For those organizations to which you anticipate being a major donor you have several options. After discussing with a group how your gift might be most helpful, you can make a cash donation outright to an organization's operating or program needs or, if you have stocks that have appreciated in value, you might elect to make a gift of stock that would benefit you also by reducing taxed capital gains. (If your donation is sizable, you can leverage it by requiring it be matched by other donations in any ratio you choose. For example, you can match with $2 every $1 given by others, or vice-versa.) Rather than giving immediate operating or program income, you can give to an endowment program.

Similarly, volunteer time can be spent doing program work; for example, working a regular shift on a rape crisis hotline, at a community food bank, or as a Girl Scout leader. Or you can do organizational work, such as serving on a board of directors or on an event committee. Or you might provide in-kind services by donating professional skills, such as legal advice, graphic design, writing, etc., or material supplies such as paper or other office supplies, or computers or other machinery.

In this chapter, we explore the different philosophical and spiritual approaches to giving that might help you decide how you're going to sort out the choices of how you want to give of your financial resources. In the next chapter, we look at the world of volunteering.

## A Legacy of Giving

The tradition of compassion through giving and service is celebrated in all religions and cultures, not only as an act of benevolence, but as a way to bring peace, justice and a sense of prosperity among people. Giving of your time and money is more than simply doing good. It is a conscious, intentional act to weave oneself into a caring culture.

Giving part of your income or assets, whether it is easy to do or a financial stretch, and giving a portion of your time out of a desire to share and help, are gifts that extend not only to the recipient, but back to the giver as well. We believe that those of us who do not give, or who do not give at our real capacity, are missing out on a joyful, wise and heartfelt experience. Moreover, if society is to reflect the real pluralism that exists around us, it is absolutely critical that we share our good fortune through compassionate action.

On the other hand, almost everyone has some anxiety about whether they have enough money, particularly whether they can "afford" to give some of it away. Likewise, our time seems ever more precious and scarce.

Our attitudes towards these resources of money and

time are formed early. The income our families did or did not have as well as messages we received about how we use money and time while we were growing up become both conscious and not-so-conscious beliefs and attitudes when we are grown. The socioeconomic class in which we were raised, the class backgrounds of our parents and extended families, and the class that we would currently describe ourselves as falling within all exert enormous influences on how we think about money. For example, if you grew up in a household where there wasn't always enough money for essentials like food and clothing, you may still be anxious about having enough food and clothing, regardless of how much income you have now. If your parents volunteered in church activities or community programs, you may be more comfortable with the idea of donating time to a cause than someone whose background didn't provide such a model.

One way to reduce your anxiety around money is to think about the beliefs you hold about it. Do you feel, for example, that you have more or less than your share (see Exercise 9), or that you may not have enough in the future? Do you believe that you can or do earn enough money to support yourself and any family dependents who may need your help? Your answers to these questions may help you articulate more specifically what you're anxious about (and therefore

## Some Facts on Net Worth in the U.S.

- Americans with incomes of $14,768 or less (the bottom 20 percent) have, on average, assets of –$7,075 (they are on average $7,075 in debt), whereas the top 20 percent (making $68,015 or more) have, on average, assets of $871,463.
- Those with the top 20 percent of assets control 80 percent of the wealth in the U.S.
- The wealthiest 1 percent of Americans have more wealth (35 percent of the total) than the bottom 92 percent combined (32 percent of the total).

what the next step is), or show you that your beliefs can override your fears.

Another way to address your feelings about how much you have and how much you want to give is to articulate your values and beliefs about living compassionately in the world. Some of us were raised with, or now follow, a religious tradition that clearly spells out the role of giving money and time within a set of spiritual values or practices. We describe here the major philosophies of giving, some spiritually based, some not. Use them to help you develop or refine your own philosophy of giving to guide you. Then use Exercise 10 to determine how much you want to give.

---

Exercise 9     **HOW MUCH MONEY DO YOU REALLY HAVE?**     5 minutes

Most of us have a distorted idea of where we fall on the nation's economic scale. Check out your relative financial situation in the following short quiz.

**My household income is... (check one)**

☐ less than $25,000 (35.8 percent of the population)

☐ $25,000–$34,999 (13.7 percent of the population)

☐ $35,000–$49,999 (16.3 percent of the population)

☐ $50,000–$74,999 (17.8 percent of the population)

☐ $75,000–$99,999 (8.2 percent of the population)

☐ $100,000 or more (8.2 percent of the population)

   ☐ *$119,540 or more (5 percent of the population)*

   ☐ *income in excess of $330,000 annually and net worth of $2.5 to $3 million (top 1 percent of the population)*

No matter what your income, if you earn any money at all, you have more money than one billion people in the world. Worldwide, average annual per capita income is $800.

## STEWARDSHIP

Many people believe they're merely shepherds of the money they earn or inherit and have a responsibility to use their money for the public good. This philosophy is based on the belief that claiming ownership of wealth reinforces the unequal power structures that enable just a few people to accumulate large amounts of money. Some who subscribe to this philosophy keep only enough money to cover their basic living expenses and give the remainder away. Notably, a number of people who inherited large amounts of money have given away all but enough to live an average comfortable life. For some inspired reading about these donors, see *We Gave Away a Fortune* by Christopher Mogil and Anne Slepian.

## TITHING

Long held as a practice in many religions, tithing means giving away one-tenth of your income (a tithe is literally one-tenth). This practice is based on the belief that only 90 percent of what you earn (or inherit) actually belongs to you and the rest must be used for the good of humanity. This is similar to the notion of stewardship, but with a specific formula for guidance. Many people like the idea of basing their giving on a percentage of their income, but choose less (or, in some cases, more) than 10 percent as their benchmark. In Judaism, the notion of tithing is expressed as *Tzedakah*, Hebrew for "righteous giving." In Islam, this same practice is called *Zakat*. As in other religions, 10 percent is expected from all.

## WORKPLACE GIVING

Many donors participate in workplace giving campaigns whereby charitable donations are deducted regularly from employees' paychecks. The system is most often administered by and benefiting a federation of agencies. Contributions can be made to a general pool or designated for specific member organizations or for particular issue or interest areas.

---

### *Alternative Workplace Giving Funds*

More than 208 alternative funds expand access for donors within workplaces who are interested in the democratization of philanthropy with an emphasis on community-based giving. Funds solicit for their member agencies or grantees which include health agencies, community development organizations, neighborhood groups, arts and cultural organizations, women's groups, African American, Hispanic, Asian American and gay/lesbian groups. The alternative funds movement is growing rapidly—it expanded by 27 percent between 1991 and 1996, while United Way's growth in employee contributions for the same period was only 4.2 percent.

If your workplace doesn't have payroll deduction giving options, we urge you to call your local alternative fund or United Way. Be sure that whatever plan you sign up for includes groups that match your values and perspectives on social reform. If not, ask for more choice in the programs being offered. (See the Resource Section for the National Alliance for Choice in Giving, which can give you more information about environmental funds, Black United Funds, Women's Funds and Social Action Funds in your area.) If you are a government employee giving through a federated campaign you may have several issue-oriented groups as options.

---

United Way has been the largest and best-known fundraising federation, focusing primarily on human service needs.

More recently, alternative funds have entered this arena and are not only building good track records but also raising money at a rate higher than United Way (see box). Many donors embrace workplace giving as a method of fulfilling their desires to give a percentage of their income without having to call on the discipline of making individual contributions from home. Other donors see their payroll deductions as a small piece of their entire giving plan. Also, because donations are spread out over the year's payroll

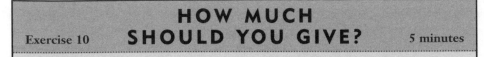
On average, Americans give away only about 2 percent of their income to charity. As mentioned in the Introduction, however, we know that many people give significantly more than that.

In thinking about what percentage of income you want to give away, you might start by looking at the chart below. Find your income level, then look across the row until you see an amount that feels comfortable to you as an amount to give away. Look at the top of the chart to see what percentage that is. Do both the amount and the percentage feel right to you? If not, where is the disparity? If you have given in the past, what percentage of your income does your past giving represent? How does it compare with the amount or percentage you chose on the chart?

| IF YOUR INCOME IS | AND YOU WANT TO GIVE | | | | | |
|---|---|---|---|---|---|---|
| | 2% | 3% | 5% | 10% | 15% | 20% |
| $30,000 | 600 | 900 | 1,500 | 3,000 | 4,500 | 6,000 |
| $40,000 | 800 | 1,200 | 2,000 | 4,000 | 6,000 | 8,000 |
| $50,000 | 1,000 | 1,500 | 2,500 | 5,000 | 7,500 | 10,000 |
| $60,000 | 1,200 | 1,800 | 3,000 | 6,000 | 9,000 | 12,000 |
| $75,000 | 1,500 | 2,250 | 3,750 | 7,500 | 11,250 | 15,000 |
| $100,000 | 2,000 | 3,000 | 5,000 | 10,000 | 15,000 | 20,000 |
| $150,000 | 3,000 | 4,500 | 7,500 | 15,000 | 22,500 | 30,000 |
| $200,000 | 4,000 | 6,000 | 10,000 | 20,000 | 30,000 | 40,000 |
| $250,000 | 5,000 | 7,500 | 12,500 | 25,000 | 37,000 | 50,000 |

*Note: You may choose your level of giving based on your pretax or post-tax figures.*

This year I/we want to give $_____, which represents _____ percent of my/our income.

Next year I/we want to give $_____, which represents _____ percent of my/our income.

periods and come from money the employee never actually has in hand, many use this method to give a sizable amount over the course of a year.

### GIVING AWAY PRINCIPAL

Although not a giving philosophy per se, "never touch principal" has been such a time-honored belief among people with inherited or earned wealth that it deserves a mention here. In addition to those mentioned above who have given away most of their assets, today some who have inherited or earned wealth are choosing to use a portion of their assets as a resource for giving during their lifetime. These assets include stocks, bonds, real estate, insurance policies or works of art. Given the intricacies of tax benefits for gifts of cash, appreciated assets and planned gifts, you might want to work with a financial planner, or estate or tax professional to consider just how much is possible or advantageous for you to give.

## *Tax-Deductibility*

- To itemize donations to nonprofits of more than $250, get a receipt with your name as donor, the date of the gift, and the amount given and keep for your tax records.
- Check with a tax advisor for the deductibility of itemized volunteer or out-of-pocket and travel expenses and what receipts are required.
- Gifts of appreciated stock, property and cash have various beneficial tax advantages; check with a tax advisor.
- No one will benefit more from your IRAs upon your death than a nonprofit (due to complex taxes upon death). List your favorite groups as beneficiaries of this part of your estate at least.

# Thinking a Little Bigger

Imagine a 28-year-old who gave $3,000 each year until she died at age 91. In 63 years of lifetime giving, she would have given $189,000, not including any gifts that came from her estate after she died. Use the following brief exercise to calculate your potential lifetime giving.

---

**Exercise 11**      **HOW MUCH WILL YOU GIVE DURING YOUR LIFETIME?**     5 minutes

Think for a moment of how much money you gave to nonprofits last year or, if you prefer, start with the figure you decided to give in Exercise 10. Now multiply that amount by the number of years you expect to live (for example, if your life expectancy is 88 and you are 48 now, multiply your giving by 40 years). Add to that an estimate of how much you've given away in your life before now, plus a percentage of your estate (10–50 percent) to nonprofits you care about.

$ _____  ×  _____
YOUR AVERAGE ANNUAL GIVING    LIFE EXPECTANCY YEARS FROM NOW

\+ $ _____  = $ _____
TOTAL AMOUNT YOU    TOTAL LIFETIME GIVING
HAVE GIVEN UP TO NOW

\+ $ _____
ESTATE GIFTS (ESTIMATE)

---

Isn't it wonderful to consider the impact you could have with all that money? Now let's look at how much time you could also contribute.

# SIX

# Volunteering and Skill Sharing

## Time Is Also a Resource

### GIVING BACK: MARGARET E. OLSEN, M.D.

My mother was a nurse and my father was born poor but became successful. They both believed in helping the next person and I carry that on. I'm a dermatologist and mother of two. Aside from my private medical practice, I volunteer about 20 hours a month for the profession. In fact, I find that my volunteer position—teaching beginning medical students how to approach patients, deal with ethical dilemmas and personality conflicts and not to be intimidating—is really my most significant work. I get the students at the very beginning, while they're still impressionable, so I have the chance to personalize medicine, give it a human face. I complain every time I go, thinking I'm not appreciated, and every time I come back enriched.

I'm also a spokesperson for the American Cancer Society, giving talks about skin cancer to Rotary Clubs and lifeguards. And before and after marathons I volunteer to give skin cancer screenings for overexposure to the sun. My position as Chief of Dermatology at the hospital is a volunteer position, and I also serve on volunteer committees there to hash out problems the hospital is having.

Last year I agreed to join the Advisory Committee of the Dermatology Foundation Leaders Society to help with fundraising for research grants. My job is to ask fellow dermatologists and corporations to donate $1,000 to $25,000 each and then to ask ten more people. The Dermatology Foundation gives us fundraising training.

I am a firm believer that you can do everything, but not at the same time; you have to choose. I believe it's easier to give money than time. Anybody can give money; it takes a little more soul to give time. I do it because I want people to have a better quality of life, to be less fearful of their own medical problems, less fearful of the doctor–patient experience. I want all these people to pass that on, to have responsibility to help the next person.

## Contributing through Volunteering

The tradition of volunteerism has a long history in this country. The organizations engaged in the work of making the world a better place almost always need people's time as much as their money. But volunteering is not growing at the rate it must to keep up with the need, a phenomenon we can ill afford.

We all know how precious time is but we're often unhappy with where our time goes. Think about whether you're satisfied with the way you spend your time. Does it accurately reflect your values? Consider where you currently put your 24 hours a day, perhaps by thinking back over the last few days or weeks. Are there adjustments you'd like to make to align your passions with the amount of time you devote to them? Would volunteering some time remind you of what you have to contribute?

Volunteering your time on behalf of a cause or group you believe in can be just as valuable and rewarding as writing a check. And while volunteering is not a substitute for the cash nonprofits need to keep the lights on and the rent paid, it's another way of giving and full of its own rewards.

If you've never been a volunteer, you may find it hard to believe that spending a few hours a week or month can make any real difference. But call your local volunteer center and ask them. Talk to friends, colleagues or family members who have volunteered. (Remember, most Americans volunteer an average of 4.2 hours a week.) What you'll almost certainly discover is that volunteers tend to be hopeful people, full of faith and creative expression about their lives and the future of their communities.

Whether you're donating your time and skills to a small or large nonprofit, your participation in and support of the nonprofit sector makes a vital contribution to society. If you choose to involve more than just your money, you'll find a world that offers opportunities for skill building, social involvement and deep satisfaction.

*Your greatest opportunities for learning and building self esteem are in pursuing what you're really good at. This holds true for your role as a giver as well as in any other part of your life. It seems simple, but is often hard to remember and even more difficult to put into practice. It is perfectly fine to pursue those things you're good at or want to learn. Don't*

## What the Nonprofit World Offers

- A place where beginners can feel useful and that welcomes a range of skills, including simple elbow-grease
- An appreciation of diversity
- A learning environment with explicit social values and a commitment to expressing them
- A place to experiment with program, product and services, where outcomes, not profit, are the motivators
- Opportunities to meet people with shared values
- A culture that integrates passion, creativity and practical needs
- Structures that may challenge and question traditional hierarchy and systems of power
- The satisfaction of seeing donations of money and time create change
- A place where skilled volunteers have influence

*get caught up in beliefs like: "I should be able to do X"; or "Everybody knows how to do Y but me." Whatever my internal messages and fears of not being skilled enough to work with others and pull off the ideal project, I want to belong and be part of a culture committed to change.*

—DOUG MALCOLM

Use the two exercises in this chapter to focus in on what you want to offer—and learn—through volunteering, and where you might want to donate some of your time.

# GIVING AND LEARNING THROUGH VOLUNTEERING

In 1994, 93 million Americans volunteered in nonprofit organizations, giving a total of more than 20 billion hours. Getting involved in any role, from stuffing envelopes to chairing board meetings, not only increases your connection to a particular organization, it often increases your understanding of the nonprofit world and your joy in giving.

If you would like to volunteer, a key step is assessing what skills you have to offer and what you would like learn. In Chapter Two you thought about what talents you could offer nonprofits. Below is a more detailed list of skills often valued. Since volunteering offers opportunities to learn as well as to give, use this exercise to define skills you would like to acquire as well as those you can share.

Put a check mark in the box after each skill in one of the three columns. This list will be helpful in finding a volunteer position in which you're both well-used and challenged.

| | GOOD AT IT | WANT TO LEARN | NOT INTERESTED |
|---|---|---|---|
| **Verbal communication** | | | |
| Conflict resolution | ☐ | ☐ | ☐ |
| Giving effective feedback | ☐ | ☐ | ☐ |
| Listening and interviewing skills | ☐ | ☐ | ☐ |
| **Office work** | | | |
| Answering phones or making calls | ☐ | ☐ | ☐ |
| Using computers | ☐ | ☐ | ☐ |
| Designing Web sites and updating Internet access | ☐ | ☐ | ☐ |
| **Finances** | | | |
| Bookkeeping | ☐ | ☐ | ☐ |
| Planning and reviewing budgets | ☐ | ☐ | ☐ |
| Preparing useful financial reports | ☐ | ☐ | ☐ |
| **Fundraising** | | | |
| Hosting a house party or other event | ☐ | ☐ | ☐ |
| Researching grant sources | ☐ | ☐ | ☐ |
| Writing grant proposals | ☐ | ☐ | ☐ |
| Asking individuals for money | ☐ | ☐ | ☐ |
| **Organizational development** | | | |
| Designing organizational policies | ☐ | ☐ | ☐ |
| Program planning and development | ☐ | ☐ | ☐ |
| Public relations and marketing | ☐ | ☐ | ☐ |
| Volunteer leadership | ☐ | ☐ | ☐ |
| Facilitating meetings | ☐ | ☐ | ☐ |
| Public speaking | ☐ | ☐ | ☐ |
| Training / teaching others a skill | ☐ | ☐ | ☐ |
| Graphic design | ☐ | ☐ | ☐ |
| **Other:**_____ | ☐ | ☐ | ☐ |

# ANALYSIS OF CURRENT VOLUNTEERING

In the chart below, list each group to which you donated time in the last twelve months, how much time you gave, what you did to assist the group, and why you chose to volunteer for that particular group.

| ORGANIZATIONS VOLUNTEERED WITH IN THE LAST 12 MONTHS | NUMBER OF HOURS | WHAT I DID | WHY I VOLUNTEERED FOR THIS GROUP |
|---|---|---|---|
| | | | |
| | | | |
| | | | |
| | | | |
| | | | |
| | | | |
| | | | |
| | | | |
| | | | |

TOTAL HOURS DONATED: _____     AVERAGE PER WEEK: _____

**Reflection:**

1. What is the relationship between your giving and your volunteering? Do you volunteer for groups that address your priority issue areas? Why or why not?

2. How do you feel about the balance between what you give and what you receive from volunteering? Do you feel your time and skills are used well? Are you getting the satisfaction or other rewards you hoped for?

3. If you could design your volunteering to have the greatest impact on issues you care about it, how might it change?

4. If you could design your volunteering to bring you the greatest personal satisfaction, how might it change?

# What You Can Expect and What's Expected of You

In return for giving, you can and should expect a lot of satisfaction, joy and learning. These are not myths. Neither is the feeling of abundance that accompanies giving your time and your money. As in any kind of relationship, however, you are entering into a contract. When you volunteer your time, you are expected to communicate what you need and want, listen to and respect the people to whom you are giving, and follow through on your commitments to them. As you can see from the Volunteer Bill of Rights that follows, you are also entitled to good direction and support.

## THE VOLUNTEER'S RIGHTS AND RESPONSIBILITIES

### It is Your Right

To be assigned a job that is worthwhile and challenging with freedom to use existing skills or develop new ones.

To be trusted with confidential information that will help you carry out your assignment.

To be kept informed through house organs, attendance at staff meetings, memoranda, etc. about what is going on in your organization.

To receive orientation training and supervision for the job you accept and to know why you are asked to do a particular job.

To expect that your time will not be wasted by lack of planning, coordination or cooperation within your organization.

To know whether your work is effective and how it can be improved: to have a chance to increase understanding of yourself, others and your community.

### It is Your Responsibility

*To accept an assignment of your choice with only as much responsibility as you can handle.*

*To respect confidences of your sponsoring organization and those of the recipients of your services.*

*To fulfill your commitment or notify your supervisor early enough that a substitute can be found.*

*To follow guidelines established by organization, codes of dress, decorum, etc.*

*To decline work not acceptable to you; not let biases interfere with job performance; not proselytize or pressure recipient to accept your standards. To use time wisely and not interfere with performance of others.*

*To continue only as long as you can be useful to recipient.*

### It is Your Right

To indicate when you do not want to receive telephone calls or when out-of-pocket costs are too great for you.

To be reimbursed for out-of-pocket costs, if it is the only way you can volunteer.

To declare allowable non-reimbursed out-of-pocket costs for federal (some state and local) income tax purposes if serving with a charitable organization.

To expect valid recommendation and encouragement from your supervisor so you can move to another job—paid or volunteer.

To be given appropriate recognition in the form of awards, certificate of achievement, etc., but even more important, recognition of your day-to-day contributions by other participants in the volunteering relationship.

To ask for a new assignment within your organization.

### It is Your Responsibility

*To refuse gifts or tips, except when recipient makes or offers something of nominal value as a way of saying "thank you."*

*To stipulate limitations: what out-of-pocket costs you can afford, when it is convenient to receive calls from organization or recipient.*

*To use reasonable judgment in making decisions when there appears to be no policy or policy not communicated to you—then, as soon as possible, consult with supervisor for future guidance.*

*To provide feedback, suggestions and recommendations to supervisor and staff if these might increase effectiveness of program.*

*To be considerate, respect competencies and work as a member of a team with all staff and other volunteers.*

Courtesy of San Francisco Volunteer Center

# One of the Most Important Contributions You Can Make

*Fundraising is the gentle art of teaching the joy of giving.*
—HENRY A. ROSSO, FOUNDER, THE FUNDRAISING SCHOOL

Even if you do not wish to make fundraising your career, we urge you to seriously consider adding this skill to your set of tools. You can take fundraising classes through a local nonprofit management center or training center. You'll learn more about how the nonprofit world works and increase your contribution to that work immensely. Assisting with fundraising is one of the most important contributions you can make to the nonprofit community.

Here's an inspiring story of one activist who decided she could do much more for the causes she believed in by learning about fundraising.

Tatjana Loh was a biologist who wanted to help raise money for battered women's shelters. Realizing she would need training in fundraising, she decided the best way to learn was a hands-on approach. Tatjana was able to volunteer several hours each week as assistant to the executive director of a local nonprofit. There she helped with fundraising tasks while learning the basic skills of the job.

She then became an intern with a battered women's shelter where she received training on how to write grants and plan events. Though these two learning experiences required a good deal of Tatjana's time, her commitment paid off because she became an excellent fundraiser. She went on to a position as executive director of a coalition of battered women's shelters, raising more than $150,000 a year.

Over the years, and because she took the time to learn a much-needed skill, her value to the nonprofit sector as a volunteer on committees, boards and as a staff person has skyrocketed.

# SEVEN

# Your Personal Giving Plan

You have now reached the heart of *Inspired Philanthropy*—writing your Personal Giving Plan. Let's review what you've done so far. You've been introduced to the world of philanthropy, the who and why of giving, the differences between traditional and inspired philanthropy and the benefits of being an organized giver. You've taken an inventory of your current position as a donor or potential donor, identified your passions as a giver and written your personal mission statement. You've assessed how you currently spend your time and money and, given your interests and vision, how you would like to allocate those resources in the future.

Now it's time to develop a philanthropic line-item in your budget or asset allocation plan and identify how, where, and when to distribute the funds you've decided to contribute. (Even if you don't have a formal budget, Exercise 10 should have given you a sense of how much you want to give, either as an absolute figure or as a percentage of your annual income.) In this chapter, you'll also create your own funding cycles, that is, decide when during the year you want to make funding decisions.

When you've created and tried out your Personal Giving Plan you'll find that it not only helps you manage your planned contributions, it also allows you to anticipate unexpected requests as well as engage in spontaneous acts of whimsy or demonstrations of caring. A Personal Giving Plan can also help you organize your time, so that you spend it in ways that reflect your values.

## The Worksheet

In the following pages you'll find a Giving Plan worksheet and examples of completed plans. You may want to make a few copies of the blank worksheet to work from or create one for yourself on a computer so you can generate copies as you need them. Spend some time looking at the sample completed forms, then try filling one out yourself, guided by the explanations below. This is one of the most important exercises in this book, so give it your complete attention.

The following pages explain each section of the form in detail. The first time through, just do it as an exercise, without necessarily committing yourself to the results. Try to fill out every column in one session. By doing this you'll find out where you need more information or aren't yet ready to make decisions. You may find you need to refer back to earlier chapters or do more research on your own.

Once you've fill in any gaps in your thinking as best you can, fill out a clean copy of the Giving Plan, creating a working document you can use.

# YOUR GIVING PLAN

The plan you create should cover one year, starting now. Once you have a plan drafted, try it out for the whole twelve months and then evaluate and refine as necessary. Use a copy of the blank Giving Plan worksheet on page 46 to do this exercise.

## 1. Your mission.
Write your mission statement from Chapter Four at the top of your funding plan.

## 2. Your total giving amount.
Write the amount of money you've decided to give (refer to Exercise 10) and the amount of time you plan to volunteer.

## 3. How will it happen? Areas of funding and volunteering.
Write your top three issue areas from Chapter Two (page 17) in the first column of the worksheet. If there are other areas you want to include, add them. You can also include a miscellaneous or whimsy category for spontaneous gifts, gifts to family and friends and tickets to fundraising events and dinners if these are part of your social, professional or political life. We recommend choosing no more than five areas of funding. Beyond that it's difficult to maintain focus and attention.

Within your miscellaneous category, give yourself room to respond to good work and urgent needs that may require a quick reaction. There are moments in history when we are simply called to consider different approaches or engage in spontaneous acts of heartfelt (inspired) giving. These are instances when timing and societal change converge. For example, if violence were to break out in a neighborhood near you, you might want to make a donation to help support conflict resolution efforts, or volunteer some hours if you have skills that could help.

## 4. How much to give? Percentages, dollar figures, and hours.
From the total amount of money you've decided to donate, allocate a percentage to each area, based on your assessment of the importance of each to your mission. Then translate each percentage into a dollar amount.

For example, in the sample giving plan on page 47, this family's strongest interest is in civil rights, so they allocate 41 percent of their giving budget to civil rights groups. They're also concerned about death and dying and alternative medical and spiritual care, so 29 percent of their giving goes to organizations whose missions are in this area. Their final area of interest is educational opportunity and support, so they give 30 percent of their financial donations to literacy and other educational endeavors. Their volunteer time is also allocated among their three interest areas.

In the column for time, write in a number of hours per week or month you would like to donate as a volunteer. This can include school volunteer time, board or volunteer committee work, or a few hours organizing a neighborhood meeting.

## 5. Who to give to? Specific groups or questions to research.
In the next column, write down names of specific organizations that you know you want to support in each area. The goals of the groups you choose should help accomplish your own giving mission. Write question marks in areas where you don't yet know of organizations to fund. Think here about the balance of small, medium and large organizations and the distribution of local, statewide, regional, national and international groups. This one step will immediately help you to deal with the many requests that come in the mail or on the phone. If a request would fit in this column, consider it. If it doesn't, but it still speaks to one of your values, consider whether you want to give to it through your whimsy fund. If neither is the case, throw it away.

For a discussion of how to identify and evaluate which groups to give to, see Chapter Eight.

*Exercise 14 continued from previous page…*

## 6. Dollar amounts per group.

If there's more than one group you want to give to in a given area, think about how you want to distribute the amount of money you've allocated to this area among the groups you've listed. There are some strategic points to consider for each organization. Would your dollars be most effective to the organization in a large or small gift? If you can make a large gift, $250 to $5,000 may be crucial to the survival of some fledgling organizations. For some colleges and high schools with multi-million-dollar capital campaigns, alumnae/alumni participation at any level may be more important than the size of the gift. A local group may do more with $100 than a national organization can do with $500.

Experiment with different amounts, and give yourself permission to make mistakes with gifts. If you learn that something you did wasn't right, you'll find out more clearly what does suit you.

## 7. Your funding cycles.

When are you going to make your funding decisions and write your checks? Will you do it once, twice or four times a year, and when do those times fall? Or will you decide whenever asked? In choosing your cycles you might consider times of the year you have a tight cash flow, tax time, heavy request times, and times when dinners and events seem to cluster. Once you've decided when you'll give, give yourself permission not to do anything outside of your giving cycles. Write the date of your funding cycles at the top of a column, then write in when you plan to write a check or otherwise give to a group. At the end of the year, reevaluate to see that you gave to all the groups and areas that you intended to. For volunteer work, decide if you're going to volunteer on a regular basis—say, a weekly stint answering phones or attending a monthly board meeting—or a seasonal basis—say, planning a fundraising event or helping write grant proposals in the fall and spring.

## 8. Notes.

Use this column to note names of contacts, previous gifts you made to this group, or other information pertinent to your gifts of money and time.

## *Congratulations!*

You have completed your first year's Giving Plan. Take a look at it and see how it feels. Make any adjustments you want before you start implementing it, then make a commitment to yourself to follow the plan for the next year.

# WORKSHEET: YOUR PERSONAL GIVING PLAN

**Mission Statement:** _____

_____

_____

**Total Giving Plan for** _____ **(year)**—*Financial donations:* _____

*Volunteering:* _____

| AREA OF FUNDING | PERCENTAGE | AMOUNT | SPECIFIC GROUPS OR QUESTIONS TO RESEARCH | AMOUNT PER GROUP | VOLUNTEER HOURS | FUNDING CYCLE DATE | NOTES, CONTACTS, PREVIOUS GIFTS |
|---|---|---|---|---|---|---|---|
| | | | | | | | |
| | | | | | | | |
| | | | | | | | |
| | | | | | | | |
| | | | | | | | |

# SAMPLE FAMILY GIVING PLAN—$8,400

**Mission Statement**—We seek to help others and ourselves through one-on-one service and teaching. We support nonprofits that help people take care of their own lives and change the conditions of poverty. We promote understanding about illness and death through work and service with the sick and dying.

**Total Giving Plan in 1999**—*Financial donations:* $8,400 (7% of our family pretax Income of $120,000). *Volunteering:* 4 hours of volunteer work together (including the kids) per week (about 800 hours this year).

| AREA OF FUNDING | PERCENTAGE | AMOUNT | SPECIFIC GROUPS OR QUESTIONS TO RESEARCH | AMOUNT PER GROUP | VOLUNTEER HOURS | FUNDING CYCLE DATE | NOTES, CONTACTS, PREVIOUS GIFTS |
|---|---|---|---|---|---|---|---|
| Civil Rights | 41% | $3450 | • NAACP | $ 500 | | 1/99 | |
| | | | • Black United Fund | $2080 | | all year | $40/week x 52 weeks from payroll deduction |
| | | | • Southern Poverty Law Center | $ 450 | | 9/99 | |
| | | | • Sorority : Delta Sigma Theta | $ 370 | 200 | 1/99 | For anti-racism film |
| | | | • Center for Democratic Renewal | $  50 | | 1/99 | Newsletter subscription |
| Death and Dying; Alternative and Spiritual Care | 29% | $2450 | • Atlanta Hospice | $ 500 | | 1/99 | In honor of Eulenia Heinz |
| | | | • Make-a-Wish Foundation | $ 250 | | 10/99 | |
| | | | • Commonwheel Center | $ 500 | 200 | 10/99 | In memory of Nellie Lorance |
| | | | • Center for Alternative Treatment & Care | $1200 | | 10/99 | $25/week for service and care |
| Educational Opportunity and Support | 30% | $2500 | • Literacy Education Fund of Atlanta | $1500 | 100 | 1/99 | Literacy volunteers during summer |
| | | | • Waldorf School Scholarship Fund | $ 300 | 200 | 10/99 | Volunteer 3 hours/wk in class, on board 4 hours/month |
| | | | • It's Elementary—film about educating kids about gay issues | $ 500 | | 2/99 | In honor of Ed's sister, principal of Everitt Jr. High |
| | | | • Mothers Against Drunk Drivers | $  50 | | 1/99 | Membership |
| | | | • Ebenezer Baptist Church | $ 150 | 100 | 10/99 | |

# SAMPLE INDIVIDUAL GIVING PLAN—$2,050

**Mission Statement** —I believe that education fosters personal growth. I aim to fund individuals, including nonprofit leaders, and provide tuition funding for educational or renewal opportunities.

**Total Giving Plan for 1999**—*Financial donations:* $2,050 to nonprofits, $1,000 to political activities and $500 in value of donated items. This totals just over 5% of my income ($41,000). *Volunteering:* Adriana to donate 150 hours at the kids' school and the Public Radio. (Average about 4 hrs per week.)

| AREA OF FUNDING | PERCENTAGE | AMOUNT | SPECIFIC GROUPS OR QUESTIONS TO RESEARCH | AMOUNT PER GROUP | VOLUNTEER HOURS | FUNDING CYCLE DATE | NOTES, CONTACTS, PREVIOUS GIFTS |
|---|---|---|---|---|---|---|---|
| Retreats for leaders, low-income people, friends | 34% | $700 | • Vallecitos Retreat Ctr. | $250 | | 3/99 | Gift to Jane's Cultural Center in '98 and to RW Awards |
| | | | • Vallecitos Retreat Ctr. | $250 | | 3/99 | For Bertilda Saenz |
| | | | • Spirit Rock Retreat for Otis Stewart | $100 | | 10/99 | Loan books for workshop as requested |
| | | | • Omega Retreat for Alice Reel (filmmaker) | $100 | | 11/99 | Gave $500 scholarship to Women Make Movies, in '97; Pledged $350 in '00 for another filmmaker |
| Leadership development and mentorship training | 24% | $500 | • Colorado Women's Foundation | $300 | | 3/99 | Community funding panel will choose groups |
| | | | • The Bean Project | $100 | | 3/99 | Talked with KD, director, on 5/99 |
| | | | • Global Fund for Women | $100 | | 11/99 | Pledged $500 for '00 |
| Education and scholarships for individuals | 17% | $350 | • Scholars Fund at International Exchange | $250 | | 4/99 | Request from Cindy Ewing |
| | | | • Hesperian Foundation | $100 | | 11/99 | Request from P. Robert for printing booklet in Spanish |
| | | | • Kids' school | | 100 | | |
| Donor's Whim: Miscellaneous Gifts, Social Events | 24% | $500 | • UM class gift for international student fund | $200 | | 3/99 | Call class rep re: challenge for scholarship fund |
| | | | • Community Arts summer youth program | $150 | | 7/99 | |
| | | | • AIDS Walkathon | $ 50 | 48 | 7/99 | Volunteer 4 hours per month on phones |
| | | | • Colorado Public Radio event/auction | $100 | 50 | 11/99 | |
| Political Gifts— Non-deductible | | $500 | • Wellstone for President | $250 | | 3/99 | |
| | | | • Bennett for Mayor | $250 | | | Local candidate |
| Political Gifts— Deductible | | $500 | • Emily's List to get out the women's vote | $250 | | 5/99 | Tax-deductible as education |
| | | | • Democratic Party | $250 | | 4/99 | |
| In-kind Gifts | | | • Habitat for Humanity | $250 (VALUE) | 200 | 5/99 | Materials; Gave $500 to national Habitat for Humanity in '97 and $500 for house plan in '98 |
| | | | • Clothes to yard sale for women's shelter | $150 (VALUE) | | 5/99 | |
| | | | • Auction item for River Project | $100 (VALUE) | | 11/99 | |

# SAMPLE FAMILY GIVING PLAN—$26,000

**Mission Statement** —We seek to encourage full participation in local agencies in the two communities in which we live (Easthampton and New York City).

**Total Giving Plan in 1999**—*Financial donations:* $26,000 (10% of family pretax income of $260,000).
*Volunteering:* 5 hours each per week of volunteer time (500 hours per year, combined).

| AREA OF FUNDING | PERCENTAGE | AMOUNT | SPECIFIC GROUPS OR QUESTIONS TO RESEARCH | AMOUNT PER GROUP | VOLUNTEER HOURS | FUNDING CYCLE DATE | NOTES, CONTACTS, PREVIOUS GIFTS |
|---|---|---|---|---|---|---|---|
| Education and Opportunity | 27% | $ 7000 | • Boys Club of New York | $4000 | 100 | 6/99 | Table at annual dinner ($1000) |
| | | | • Long Island Public Radio | $1000 | 100 | 6/99 | For summer youth intern |
| | | | • Planned Parenthood | $1000 | | 12/99 | |
| | | | • Madeline Island Library | $1000 | | 12/99 | In honor of Agnes Cadotte |
| Health | 29% | $ 7500 | • Southampton Hospital | $2000 | | 6/99 | In honor of John |
| | | | • Lighthouse for the Blind | $1000 | | 6/99 | |
| | | | • Long Island Food Bank | $1500 | | 12/99 | |
| | | | • NY Food Bank | $3000 | | 12/99 | For the storage building fund |
| Nature/Beauty/ Environment | 44% | $11,500 | • Botanical Gardens, NYC | $7500 | 300 | 1/99 | In honor of Suzie Williams |
| | | | • The Nature Conservancy | $1000 | | 1/99 | |
| | | | • Trees Foundation | $1000 | | 6/99 | In honor of Jordan's birthday |
| | | | • Central Park Foundation | $2000 | | 6/99 | |

# SAMPLE INDIVIDUAL GIVING PLAN—$45,000

**Mission Statement**—I give to preserve economic justice, the environment and accuracy of the media. I also seek to hear, see and activate diverse leadership through grantmaking to community-based foundations and grassroots groups. I intend to give ½ to national/statewide projects, ¼ to local projects, ¼ to international projects.

**Total Giving Plan in 1999**—*Financial donations:* $45,000 (10% of income=$22,500 and 1% of principal=$22,500 of $2.3 million in assets). *Volunteering:* 200 hours per year (about 5 hours per week that I am available).

| AREA OF FUNDING | PERCENTAGE | AMOUNT | SPECIFIC GROUPS OR QUESTIONS TO RESEARCH | AMOUNT PER GROUP | VOLUNTEER HOURS | FUNDING CYCLE DATE | NOTES, CONTACTS, PREVIOUS GIFTS |
|---|---|---|---|---|---|---|---|
| Environmental Education and Support | 22% | $10,000 | • Environmental Support Center | $2500 | | 6/99 | Meet with Jim Abernathy in DC |
| | | | • Save the Redwoods | $1000 | | 6/99 | |
| | | | • International Rivers | $2150 | | 10/99 | |
| | | | • Women's Forest Sanctuary | $ 500 | 20 | 11/99 | In honor of Sara |
| | | | • Chemical Impact Project | $ 750 | 20 | 11/99 | Heard at State Of World Forum |
| | | | • Global Greengrants | $2000 | | 11/99 | New: Fund for 3 years |
| | | | • National Res. Defense Council | $1000 | | 11/99 | |
| | | | • National Trust for Historic Preservation | $ 100 | | 6/99 | Membership |
| Media and Accountability | 30% | $8250 | • Inst. for Pub. Accuracy | $1250 | | 6/99 | |
| | | | • Women's Desk/F.A.I.R. | $1500 | | 6/99 | Second year of 5-year pledge |
| | | | • Media Alliance | $ 500 | | 6/99 | |
| | | | • The Progressive Media Project | $1500 | | 6/99 | |
| | | | • Public Media Center | $1000 | | 6/99 | |
| | | | • The Comm. Consortium | $1250 | | 11/99 | |
| | | | • Pacifica Radio | $ 750 | 10 | 11/99 | Asked by Jeff |
| | | | • KPFA | $ 500 | 80 | 11/99 | |
| Philanthropic Infrastructure | 28% | $12,750 | • National Network of Grantmakers | $2500 | | 11/99 | National Conference Sponsorship |
| | | | • Changemakers Project | $5000 | | 5/99 | To support awards for nonprofits |
| | | | • A Territory Resource | $1500 | | 6/99 | Outreach to business community |
| | | | • Funding Exchange | $2500 | | 6/99 | To expand donor education |
| | | | • Third Wave — Youth | $1250 | | 5/99 | Scholarships for women |
| Economic Justice | 20% | $9000 | • Highlander Center | $1000 | | 5/99 | For work in TN & KY |
| | | | • United for a Fair Economy | $2000 | 40 | 6/99 | |
| | | | • Center for 3rd World Organizing | $3000 | 20 | 4/99 | |
| | | | • Women of Color Resource Center | $1500 | 10 | 4/99 | |
| | | | • ELAN Network | $1500 | | 11/99 | Popular economics educators network |
| Donor's Whim: Miscellaneous Gifts, Social Events | 9% | $4000 | • Lambi Fund of Haiti | $1000 | | 11/99 | |
| | | | • Yo!(uth) Radio Project | $1000 | | 10/99 | Sandy Close's project |
| | | | • Center for Community Change | $1000 | | 11/99 | Dinner to honor d'Opal, Sanchez |
| | | | • Films Arts Foundation | $1000 | | 6/99 | Two films |
| Political Gifts— Nondeductible | 2% | $1000 | • Voter registration projects | $1000 | | 9/99 | |
| In-kind gifts | | $ 250 | • Clothes to Centers Project | $ 250 (VALUE) | | 6/99 | |

# MULTI-YEAR GIVING PLAN

| ORGANIZATION | 1998 | 1999 | 2000 | 2001 | 2002 | 2003 |
|---|---|---|---|---|---|---|
| Atlanta Hospice | | $ 500 | | | | |
| Black United Fund | $2000 | $2080 | | | | |
| Carter Center—Georgia Peace Corps | $ 250 | | | | | |
| Center for Alternative Treatment and Care | | $ 300 | | | | |
| Center for Democratic Renewal | | $ 50 | | | | |
| Commonwheel Center | | $ 500 | | | | |
| Ebenezer Baptist Church | $1000 | $1200 | $1200 pledge | | | |
| Habitat for Humanity | $ 150 | | | | | |
| Humane Society of America | $ 250 | | | | | |
| It's Elementary—film about educating kids about gays issues | | $ 400 | | | | |
| Literacy Education Fund of Atlanta | $1000 | $1500 | $1500 pledge | | | |
| Little Sunshine Day Care Center | $ 300 | | | | | |
| Make-a-Wish Foundation | $ 250 | $ 250 | | | | |
| Mothers Against Drunk Drivers | $ 50 | $ 50 | | | | |
| National Institute for Breast Cancer Research | | | $ 250 pledge | | | |
| NAACP | $ 500 | $ 500 | $ 500 pledge | | | |
| Sorority—Eulenia's | $ 370 | $ 370 | | | | |
| Southern Poverty Law Center | $ 450 | $ 450 | $ 500 pledge | | | |
| Spellman College—Scholarships | $ 250 | | $ 250 pledge | | | |
| St. Paul's Thrift Shop | $ 750 clothes donation | | | | | |
| Waldorf School Scholarship Fund | $ 250 | $ 250 | | | | |
| **Total Donations:** | **$7070** | **$8400** | | | | |
| **Total Donated Goods / Clothes:** | **$ 750** | | | | | |

# Clarifying Your Intention

As you begin to make your gifts, you may want to ground yourself even further in your intentions for them. Knowing what your intention is will also help later when you evaluate whether the gift was effective.

You may want to copy the worksheet on the following page so you can fill it out for each gift that you intend to evaluate (it takes only a few minutes to complete), and file it as a reminder of your own intention at the time of the giftgiving.

## WORKSHEET: GIVING INTENTION

Name of organization _____
_____

Date of gift _____     Amount of gift $ _____

With this gift/donation, I want to participate in:
☐ The spirit of generosity and faith
☐ Supporting someone I trust or respect
☐ Sustaining the mission of an organization I believe in
☐ Working with other donors or nonprofit leaders
☐ Increasing the financial capacity of an organization
☐ Helping to leverage more resources through a challenge gift
☐ Advancing leadership capacity within an organization (i.e., through money or time given expressly for trainings)
☐ Providing support for direct services to constituents
☐ Helping to provide specific outreach or support to a targeted population or a specific geographic area
☐ Assisting to ensure that the issues being addressed by this organization or leaders get media or PR exposure
☐ Providing tangible goods (clothes, computers, desks, food)
☐ Assuring public policy or advocacy linkages
☐ Designating money for research or documentation
☐ Helping a group or community do better planning/visioning/collaborating
☐ Contributing to public education options
☐ Funding an artistic presentation/interpretation or expression
☐ Attaining visibility or recognition for our family or business
☐ Other: _____

**For gifts of more than $5,000:**

1. The organization and I have set detailed goals or agreed on the expected impact of my gift:  ☐ Yes     ☐ No
*Comments/notes:*
_____
_____

2. At the time of my gift I specified how and if I wanted to be recognized.
☐ I was specific with _____ (person's name) at _____ (name of organization) about my wish to remain anonymous; we spoke on _____ (date) in person/phone/in writing (attach letter to file).
☐ I do not wish to remain anonymous.
*Comments/notes:*
_____
_____

3. I spoke with _____ (person's name) in the organization about reports I do or do not want to receive on the organization's work on _____ (date).
*Comments/notes:*
_____
_____

*Example: "I spoke with Jody Stella on July 16 about the fact that I only wish to receive the annual report and one call or visit a year."*

# Results and Impact: Giftmaking Yearly Review

There is much to learn by implementing your giving plan. Once you've completed your year of giftmaking, or as often as you want to do so, reflect on how well your money was used and how well you feel you did as a donor. The next two exercises provide questions that may be useful.

| Exercise 15 | RESULTS AND IMPACT | 10-15 minutes |
|---|---|---|

If you gave large gifts that you want to evaluate before giving again, answer the following questions about the impact of your donation:

a) What were my intentions and goals and were they reached? (Have I reviewed the organization's finances or received a report about how the money was expended? Was my donation spent as it was intended or designated or originally requested? If not, was I informed along the way?)

b) What do I perceive is the organization's progress and what tools can I use for evaluation? What other organizations collaborated or worked on this issue? What feedback could I get from them about the effectiveness of the group I gave to? (For large gifts: Do I want to hire someone to do a more formal evaluation or do it myself?)

c) How stable does the leadership seem now? Is it stronger? Weaker?

d) Is the organization more, or less, financially stable now?

e) Were there strategic outcomes—programs, products or services?

f) Did the gift leverage other money or results?

g) How do I feel about administrative costs vs. program and fundraising costs at this organization now? Are they different than I expected?

h) What learning went on for me and for the organization through this gift, if any?

*Notes about future gifts or about concerns or feedback to share with group or leader:*

# HOW YOU DID AS A DONOR

Take a few minutes to recall your giving and volunteering over the past year. Check any of the items below that describe your activities. Then go through the checklist again and put a star next to anything you would like to do differently in the coming year.

## Volunteering

**I volunteered each week/month (circle one):**

☐ 1–2 hours
☐ 3–5 hours
☐ 6–10 hours
☐ 11–16 hours
☐ 17–20 hours
☐ 21+ hours

**I volunteered with the following organizations and did the following activities:**

_____

_____

_____

_____

_____

_____

**I increased my ability to assist the nonprofit sector by:**

☐ taking a class (e.g., how to be a board member, fundraising, other skills)
☐ reading about nonprofit or community issues
☐ other: _____

_____

## Fundraising

**I leveraged my ability to support organizations by:**

☐ learning about fundraising
☐ fundraising from individuals
☐ hosting events for nonprofits or politicians
☐ co-hosting large events (e.g., buying a table of seats and organizing friends to come)
☐ speaking as a donor at events to motivate others to give
☐ speaking to media about my giving
☐ other: _____

_____

## Giving

**I gave:**

☐ small amounts to many groups
☐ larger amounts to several groups
☐ a balance of the two

**I gave to:**

☐ too many groups
☐ enough groups
☐ not enough groups

**As a percentage of income or assets I gave:**

☐ adequately
☐ less than I could have
☐ more than I could really afford

**I collected mail requests and gave to selected ones:**

☐ as they came in
☐ monthly
☐ quarterly
☐ yearly
☐ not at all

**I attended fundraising events:**

☐ once or twice
☐ quarterly
☐ monthly
☐ more often
☐ not at all

**I generally gave:**

☐ anonymously
☐ using my name
☐ publicly if asked

**I gave to the following number of issues or populations:**

☐ 1–2
☐ 3–4
☐ 5–6

**I evaluated where to give by:**

☐ reading annual reports, funding proposals, or direct mail pieces
☐ going on site visits or talking to staff
☐ attending briefings on the issues I give to
☐ talking to other funders and activists
☐ checking with groups that evaluate nonprofits
☐ listening to my heart
☐ other: _____

_____

## Planning

**I followed an overall giving plan that named how much I would give of:**

☐ income
☐ assets
☐ time

*Continued on next page*

**My giving plan specified:**
☐ my areas of focus
☐ the types of organizations and strategies I want to support

**I reflected on my overall giving:**
☐ at the beginning or end of the year
☐ on a regular basis during the year (how often?)
☐ through drawing, writing, or talking with others
☐ through a formal evaluation process

**I talked or consulted with the following people about my philanthropy:**
☐ a financial planner or investment manager
☐ an estate attorney
☐ a friend or fellow donor
☐ a mentor or philanthropic advisor

☐ a development director
☐ foundation staff
☐ an activist involved in the areas I give to
☐ a donor support network
☐ other: _____

_____

**Identity and Community**
**I let others know I am:**
☐ a donor/giver/philanthropist
☐ a volunteer or activist
☐ a donor activist or donor organizer

**I made some of my giving decisions:**
☐ with others (partner, family, friends)

☐ by talking with other donors who give to what I do
☐ with support of a donor network or giving club
☐ other: _____

_____

**Integration of Values**
**In addition to giving and volunteering, I expressed my values by:**
☐ loaning money to nonprofit organizations
☐ investing in socially responsible companies
☐ investing in community development loan funds and microenterprise funds
☐ practicing ways to live more simply
☐ other: _____

Overall I feel _____ about my giving plan and process.

Next year I want to:

_____

_____

_____

_____

# EIGHT

# Where to Give, and How

In the last chapter you drafted your Giving Plan for the next twelve months. If you had more questions than answers when considering the column of specific groups you would give to, you're not alone. How many of the more than one million nonprofits in the United States alone do we really know about? Do you only know about the big national groups that get your attention with their direct mail appeals and community billboards? What if you've decided you want to give to activities that respond to local problems in your community, or you've heard about some regional groups that sound interesting? Or maybe you're wondering if the groups you already give to are really the ones you want to continue to support?

Most of us have these questions. One of the benefits of creating your giving plan is giving yourself the time to really think about where your financial contributions will have the greatest impact on the issues you care most about.

When considering which groups you want to include in your giving, start by reviewing the list of groups you currently give to that you listed in Exercise 5 (page 19). Compare that list with your top priority interest areas from Exercise 3 (page 16). Do your gifts reflect your top interest areas? Do you wonder if there are other groups also working in these areas that you don't yet know about? Are you thinking only about local groups? Would donating to statewide or national organizations achieve other goals? You might start by asking friends, family and colleagues which organizations they support. Beyond such an informal survey, finding out about what groups exist that address the issues you care most about takes a little research.

## Finding Groups to Give To

In the human service field, in addition to any groups you already know about, you can contact your nearest United Way office or alternative fund or federation for a list of groups they fund. For issues outside of human services, your local or statewide community foundation, Funding Exchange member fund, or women's foundation or federation can provide information about groups serving your community. These organizations are helpful if you're just beginning to identify what kinds of things you might want to fund or need more information about a specific nonprofit. They can also help you structure a gift, such as through endowed or expendable funds or pooled funds, where a community funding board makes granting decisions.

You can also learn more about specific nonprofits from a growing number of private monitoring groups such as the National Charities Information Bureau, the Philanthropic Advisory Service of the Better Business Bureau, and the American Institute of Philanthropy. Each of these groups reviews financial and fiduciary performance of nonprofits.

Another source of information is Philanthropic Research, Inc., which maintains comprehensive reports on thousands of organizations. You can locate up-to-date information on these and other groups through the World Wide Web (see the Resource Section in Appendix F for contact information). See Chapter Eight for more ideas on how to find information about groups to give to.

As you focus on specific groups you think you may want to donate to, contact them for their newsletters or annual reports. An annual report will describe the agency's mission and its goals and objectives for the previous year and how they were met; it will also convey the agency's perception of its impact and effectiveness. (Many small, grassroots groups may not have an annual report.) By law, you may request a group's tax report, called a "990 Form," which will reveal the percentage of gifts and income spent on administration, program and fundraising. When considering how much of your dollar the agency should spend on fundraising and administration, keep in mind that, though the rule of thumb is not more than 25 percent for both, extenuating circumstances may require you to consider the group's situation. Start-up agencies or those doing work that has never been done, or that is high risk or complex may need up to 40 percent or even more of the charitable dollar to be spent on infrastructure at first. We urge you to focus first on the content of the work delivered (who are they serving and what is the quality of the service or product?) and then look at the budget and finances.

Getting even closer, you might want to attend events a group sponsors. Or you can volunteer with the group to get a sense of its leadership and the strength of the executive director and her or his staff, the board and their experience, or the size and structure of the volunteer corps. If you become a major donor to a group (the amount considered a major gift varies with the size of the group, from $100 to $5,000 or more) you can expect to meet with a board or staff member to receive updates about the work of the nonprofit. In an hour you can ask detailed questions and get a fairly thorough snapshot of the agency's apparent health.

If you're thinking of giving a sizable gift to an organization ($2,500 or more) you may want to conduct a site visit for an in-depth discussion of the organization's goals, leadership, fundraising and accomplishments. (See Appendix D for a list of questions you might want to ask during such a visit.)

If you're considering an even larger gift ($10,000 or more) and want to be sure of the group's stability, it's perfectly acceptable for you to ask a group's treasurer or administrative manager for help reading the financial statements contained in an annual report and to ask for current quarterly financial statements being prepared for their board. You can also ask for references to groups they collaborate with and call them for their perspective on the organization you're considering funding.

## Ways to Give: Each Serving Different Needs

Just as you're taking the time to plan where your contributions will have the greatest impact, you should also think about all the different ways you can give. Your giving will be more effective if you're specific about the ways you can give your time, talents and treasures, if you're clear about your decision-making process, and if you specify whether your giving will be part of a formal group or grant-making entity and what you'll designate your dollars in support of. The following exercise might help you think about all the different ways there are to give, and which are right for you.

# GIVING METHODS

Put a check mark in the appropriate column for each of the methods you've used or ways you could consider giving financial support.

| | I HAVE USED THIS METHOD | I WANT INFORMATION ON THIS METHOD | NOT APPLICABLE TO ME OR NOT INTERESTED |
|---|---|---|---|
| **Financial gifts** | | | |
| Written a check. . . . . . . . . . . . . . . . . . . . . . . . . . . . . . . . . . . . . . . . | ☐ | ☐ | ☐ |
| Given cash. . . . . . . . . . . . . . . . . . . . . . . . . . . . . . . . . . . . . . . . . . . . | ☐ | ☐ | ☐ |
| Donated by credit card . . . . . . . . . . . . . . . . . . . . . . . . . . . . . . . . . | ☐ | ☐ | ☐ |
| Given stock . . . . . . . . . . . . . . . . . . . . . . . . . . . . . . . . . . . . . . . . . . . | ☐ | ☐ | ☐ |
| Given through pooled funds. . . . . . . . . . . . . . . . . . . . . . . . . . . . . . | ☐ | ☐ | ☐ |
| Made a loan to a friend, nonprofit or community loan or microenterprise fund . . . | ☐ | ☐ | ☐ |
| Through charitable estate planning . . . . . . . . . . . . . . . . . . . . . . . . | ☐ | ☐ | ☐ |
| Designated insurance policies or IRAs to a nonprofit beneficiary . . . . . . . . . . . . . . | ☐ | ☐ | ☐ |
| Established charitable trusts. . . . . . . . . . . . . . . . . . . . . . . . . . . . . . . | ☐ | ☐ | ☐ |
|    –charitable remainder trust . . . . . . . . . . . . . . . . . . . . . . . . | ☐ | ☐ | ☐ |
|    –charitable lead trusts . . . . . . . . . . . . . . . . . . . . . . . . . . . . | ☐ | ☐ | ☐ |
|    –unitrusts . . . . . . . . . . . . . . . . . . . . . . . . . . . . . . . . . . . . . | ☐ | ☐ | ☐ |
|    –annuity trusts. . . . . . . . . . . . . . . . . . . . . . . . . . . . . . . . . . | ☐ | ☐ | ☐ |
|    –unified credit trusts. . . . . . . . . . . . . . . . . . . . . . . . . . . . . | ☐ | ☐ | ☐ |
|    –qualified personal residence trusts . . . . . . . . . . . . . . . . . | ☐ | ☐ | ☐ |
| Other: _____ . . . . . . . . . . . . . . . . . . . . . . | ☐ | ☐ | ☐ |
| **Non-financial gifts** | | | |
| Given house or space for fundraising events or for activists' retreat . . . . . . . . . . | ☐ | ☐ | ☐ |
| Written a letter or placed a phone call of recommendation (leverage) . . . . . . . . . | ☐ | ☐ | ☐ |
| Given equipment . . . . . . . . . . . . . . . . . . . . . . . . . . . . . . . . . . . . . . . | ☐ | ☐ | ☐ |
| Given skills. . . . . . . . . . . . . . . . . . . . . . . . . . . . . . . . . . . . . . . . . . . . | ☐ | ☐ | ☐ |
| Other: _____ . . . . . . . . . . . . . . . . . . . . . . | ☐ | ☐ | ☐ |
| **Decision making** | | | |
| By self . . . . . . . . . . . . . . . . . . . . . . . . . . . . . . . . . . . . . . . . . . . . . . | ☐ | ☐ | ☐ |
| With partner. . . . . . . . . . . . . . . . . . . . . . . . . . . . . . . . . . . . . . . . . . | ☐ | ☐ | ☐ |
| With family (multi ages). . . . . . . . . . . . . . . . . . . . . . . . . . . . . . . . . | ☐ | ☐ | ☐ |
| With groups of other people from similar incomes . . . . . . . . . . . . . . . . . . | ☐ | ☐ | ☐ |
| With mixed-income group . . . . . . . . . . . . . . . . . . . . . . . . . . . . . . . | ☐ | ☐ | ☐ |
| With group of co-workers or friends . . . . . . . . . . . . . . . . . . . . . . . . | ☐ | ☐ | ☐ |
| **Gave decision-making power to others** | | | |
| To group of activists . . . . . . . . . . . . . . . . . . . . . . . . . . . . . . . . . . . | ☐ | ☐ | ☐ |
| To a staff member, program advisor . . . . . . . . . . . . . . . . . . . . . . . . | ☐ | ☐ | ☐ |
| To someone else to decide. . . . . . . . . . . . . . . . . . . . . . . . . . . . . . . | ☐ | ☐ | ☐ |
| Other: _____ . . . . . . . . . . . . . . . . . . . . . . | ☐ | ☐ | ☐ |

*Continued on next page*

| | I HAVE USED THIS METHOD | I WANT INFORMATION ON THIS METHOD | NOT APPLICABLE TO ME OR NOT INTERESTED |
|---|:---:|:---:|:---:|
| **Mechanism** | | | |
| Giving club/civic group/sorority/fraternity . . . . . . . . . . . . . . . . . . . . . . . . . . . . . . . . . . | ☐ | ☐ | ☐ |
| To a community foundation/women's fund/Jewish Federation/Catholic Charity . . . | ☐ | ☐ | ☐ |
| To a donor-advised fund . . . . . . . . . . . . . . . . . . . . . . . . . . . . . . . . | ☐ | ☐ | ☐ |
| As part of a donors' circle . . . . . . . . . . . . . . . . . . . . . . . . . . . . . . . . . | ☐ | ☐ | ☐ |
| As part of a mixed group of low-income and wealthy activists . . . . . . . . . . . . . | ☐ | ☐ | ☐ |
| Through workplace or payroll deduction . . . . . . . . . . . . . . . . . . . . . . . . . . | ☐ | ☐ | ☐ |
| Through a family foundation . . . . . . . . . . . . . . . . . . . . . . . . . . . . . . . . . | ☐ | ☐ | ☐ |
| Other: _____ . . . . . . . . . . . . . . | ☐ | ☐ | ☐ |
| **Designation of donations** | | | |
| Operating expenses. . . . . . . . . . . . . . . . . . . . . . . . . . . . . . . . . . . . . . . . | ☐ | ☐ | ☐ |
| Capital expenses (e.g., building or equipment). . . . . . . . . . . . . . . . . . . . . . | ☐ | ☐ | ☐ |
| Leadership sabbaticals. . . . . . . . . . . . . . . . . . . . . . . . . . . . . . . . . . . . . . | ☐ | ☐ | ☐ |
| Endowment gifts . . . . . . . . . . . . . . . . . . . . . . . . . . . . . . . . . . . . . . . . . | ☐ | ☐ | ☐ |
| Matching or challenge gifts . . . . . . . . . . . . . . . . . . . . . . . . . . . . . . . . . . | ☐ | ☐ | ☐ |
| Technical assistance . . . . . . . . . . . . . . . . . . . . . . . . . . . . . . . . . . . . . . | ☐ | ☐ | ☐ |
| Scholarships . . . . . . . . . . . . . . . . . . . . . . . . . . . . . . . . . . . . . . . . . . . | ☐ | ☐ | ☐ |
| Loans. . . . . . . . . . . . . . . . . . . . . . . . . . . . . . . . . . . . . . . . . . . . . . . . | ☐ | ☐ | ☐ |
| Existing debt reduction . . . . . . . . . . . . . . . . . . . . . . . . . . . . . . . . . . . . | ☐ | ☐ | ☐ |
| **Time frame** | | | |
| One-year gift . . . . . . . . . . . . . . . . . . . . . . . . . . . . . . . . . . . . . . . . . . . | ☐ | ☐ | ☐ |
| Multi-year gift . . . . . . . . . . . . . . . . . . . . . . . . . . . . . . . . . . . . . . . . . . | ☐ | ☐ | ☐ |
| Gift with no amount of time attached . . . . . . . . . . . . . . . . . . . . . . . . . . . | ☐ | ☐ | ☐ |
| Planned gift (during lifetime or upon death) . . . . . . . . . . . . . . . . . . . . . . . | ☐ | ☐ | ☐ |

**Reflection:**

1. What is your analysis of your methods of giving:

_____

_____

_____

2. What methods do you want to learn more about:

_____

_____

_____

# NINE

# Fine-Tuning Your Giving

In learning any new skill, there are moments of frustration and feelings of ineptitude. In this chapter, we talk about the natural progression people make as they mature in their philanthropy and we address the informational, emotional and strategic barriers people face to becoming effective donors. We offer a handful of suggestions for overcoming these barriers and pushing through to the next level of inspired philanthropy.

## The Philanthropic Learning Curve

Becoming an inspired philanthropist takes time. Like any new skill or role, it follows its own trajectory, which includes exciting periods of rapid learning to frustratingly slow plateaus and time when it all just feels too hard. During these early months, it is particularly helpful to share your experiences with other donors with whom you can commiserate, and who can coach and cheer you on.

Every philanthropist enters the process of giving from a different point. Your approach to giving depends on your enthusiasm and focus, the availability of time, understanding of the issues that interest you, and your comfort with analyzing information and making decisions.

There does, however, seem to be a progression common to all philanthropists that has been dubbed by H. Peter Karoff of The Philanthropic Initiative in Boston "the philanthropic curve." The following is how he has described it.

### LEVEL ONE: Becoming a Donor

A complex combination of influences, that can include personal and religious values, family background, business and social pressures, ego, and heart-felt response to the world around you, motivates you to become a donor. Giving becomes part of your way of life, your position in the community, your yearning to be a good person. Over time, giving becomes less satisfying, requests increase. For the most part, you give small amounts to an ever-growing number of groups.

### LEVEL TWO: Getting Organized

You have enough experience as a donor to be able to analyze your giving patterns, decide what really interests you, and which gifts have awarded you the most satisfaction. You begin to develop priorities and criteria for your giving, learn to say no, and make fewer but larger grants.

### LEVEL THREE: Becoming More Strategic

Knowing what issues really interest you, you now realize that you don't know enough about them. So you do research: talking to other donors, to experts in the field, reading, consulting with your community foundation, making site visits to organizations addressing those issues. Your giving becomes more focused, the groups you support reflecting your top priorities.

### LEVEL FOUR: Focusing on Issues and Results

At this stage, you become more interested in results and evaluation. It is important that you maximize your giving and increase the possibilities that it will make a difference. Rather than responding to effects, you begin to investigate underlying causes, focusing on building the capacities of the organizations of the most talented and effective nonprofit leaders. You are more proactive, searching out the best people and organizations to support rather than waiting for requests to come to you.

### LEVEL FIVE: Leveraging

At this stage, your giving supports the development and funding of programs designed to meet specific programmatic objectives. You enter into collaborations with other donors and participate in public-private partnerships. You have become increasingly knowledgeable about the issues you fund, about what works, about what can really make a difference.

### LEVEL SIX: Harmony and Congruence

You experience a satisfying alignment between your most deeply held values and your giving interests. Your philanthropy is one of the most exciting and fulfilling aspects of your life.

## Breaking the Barriers to More Effective Giving

As with any activity—from sticking with an exercise program to learning a new language—things get in the way of our learning or growth, or our early determination gives way to frustrations that can allow us to get off track and never get back. We don't want that to happen with you and your desire to be more effective in your giving, so we present here the major barriers many encounter as they begin to organize their giving, along with some solutions for you to try. Specific organizations and networks referred to can all be found in the Resource Section, Appendix F.

---

### *A Donor's Development*

Here's how a donor named Harriet Barlow describes her development as a donor:

*I'm learning over the years what I need to stay energized and optimistic as a giver: some of my funding needs to nurture things I can literally see and touch—murals in my neighborhood, community gardens, projects that affect people I know. Some of my money needs to go towards projects shaping the larger political and economic picture, touching the lives of people I will never meet, perhaps taking longer than my lifetime to bear fruit. For instance, during the Mississippi flood disaster in 1994, I didn't give blankets and canned goods, but instead supported projects that would help people rethink how to build on flood plains.*

*I also need a balance between funding creative start-ups that get my adrenaline going, and directing my money to projects I'm confident will bring results. High-risk and low risk—like a good stock portfolio! When I evaluate my giving, I am not judging whether others have done right by me, but rather assessing my own thought process, how I might become more strategic, more deeply attuned to what I need as a giver at this stage in my life.*

---

The three major barriers to effective giving we've identified are:

- *Informational:* Lack of information about organizations and activities you might get involved in
- *Emotional:* Lack of confidence as a donor, volunteer or activist
- *Strategic:* Lack of the time, focus or support that would help you push through the other barriers

## INFORMATIONAL BARRIERS

How do I find out what organizations do the things I'm interested in supporting? What roles are possible for me to play? Where do different organizations fit into the picture of making social change?

### Solutions for Informational Barriers

The Resource Section (Appendix F) contains a wealth of information about networks and collaborating associations that can lead you to more information about who is doing what in the nonprofit world. In addition, you might:

1. Attend issue-oriented conferences or panels. Collaborating organizations such as the Women's Funding Network, the Children's Defense Fund, the American Association of Retired Persons, and the NAACP all have annual conferences at which you can learn more about the status of issues, strategies and solutions. Look in the newspaper for national or regional conferences, issue-oriented alumnae gatherings, or briefings that may be coming to your area.

2. Read the annual reports distributed by community foundations, United Way, alternative federations, private foundations, and the community groups these organizations fund or that you read about in the newspaper or hear about from friends. You may get annual reports or lists of grantees by calling agencies or foundations directly and requesting them or by visiting the library or Foundation Center in your region.

3. Subscribe to and read publications that cover news in the nonprofit world such as *The Nonprofit Times* or *The Chronicle of Philanthropy.*

4. Attend the issue briefings or workshops periodically offered by nonprofit training and research organizations and funders' associations such as the Support Centers, the Foundation Center Libraries or regional associations of grantmakers, such as the Michigan Council of Foundations, or the National Network of Grantmakers.

5. Attend fundraising events.

6. Ask friends, family, and colleagues which organizations they support.

7. Volunteer for different organizations. You can agree to volunteer for an organization for short or longer commitments. Be honest with the organization that you're seeking to find out more about them by helping them for a few hours a week over an agreed-upon number of months.

8. If you're a donor who is considering giving away more than $5,000 a year and would like the benefit of meeting with other donors to consider issues or strategies, or if you would like to consider the power of collective giving, you might want to join a donor network. Regional associations of grantmakers also have periodic programs for major donors giving $10,000+. The Council on Foundations and educational organizations such as Resourceful Women, The Philanthropic Initiative, the Third Wave Foundation and the Council on Foundation's Family Foundation program have meetings for major and family donors who give significant amounts. Call organizations that sponsor donor forums and ask them for their criteria for attendance and a copy of their publication list and meeting descriptions.

9. Write, call or visit (call first) executive directors or development directors of organizations you care about and ask what's needed, how you might help or what they perceive is a core or strategic funding or volunteer need. Most often agencies need operating income (to pay salaries, rent, lights, phone and printing) before they need money to launch a new program. Foundations historically have preferred to fund programs instead of operating expenses, so your support of the "annual fund" or core operating expenses not covered by grants really means a lot to groups.

## EMOTIONAL BARRIERS

What exactly is my role as a donor, volunteer or activist? What skills do I need to have or should I learn to fulfill this role? How can I become more comfortable with the idea of giving away what is for me large amounts of money? How can I decide what is an appropriate amount to give?

### Solutions for Emotional Barriers

1. Call the Impact Project or Resourceful Women for referrals to money therapists or family facilitators.

2. Ask friends if they know of anyone who would be a good "money mentor" or teacher.

3. Conduct informational interviews with other donors who are nonprofit leaders to learn how they organize and manage their active lives. Some questions to ask: How do you manage the organizing aspects of being a donor—what materials to keep on an organization's needs, budgets and contact you've had with them, etc.? What personal issues about money, influence and power have come up for you as a donor or fundraiser, and how do you handle the innate inequities in philanthropy between giver and fundraiser? What has helped you stay hopeful amidst the enormous task of addressing community imbalances?

## STRATEGIC BARRIERS

How can I limit my involvement in things I'm not really that passionate about? How can I feel less isolated about how I am planning and doing my giving?

### Solutions for Strategic Barriers

1. Review the values you identified in Exercise 3 (page 16). If your current activities are not connected to your top values or priorities, decide whether you want to graciously extricate yourself from them and seek activities more in line with your priorities.

2. Consider limiting your time commitments. Experiment with allocating a specific time commitment—for example one day a week, month or year—to your vocation or avocation as a donor or donor activist.

3. Practice refraining from responding to every funding request on the spot. When you receive requests in person, let people know that you'll give the request careful consideration in light of your priorities. When you receive requests in the mail, consider them in light of all the other requests you've received in a given time period and in relation to your giving plan.

4. Join a donor network (see #8 under Informational Barriers). If you want to work in community there are lots of networks from which to choose. It can be fantastic to have a dream, create an initiative and have other donors or activists join you. For some, it's too complicated a process. For others, it's a way to assure accountability, fun and others' involvement. See the next section for some examples of collaborative funding projects.

5. Be attuned to and reflect on what working style is most comfortable for you. Some people prefer to work alone, while others feel they get better and more diverse information by connecting with others. Some donors love to create collaborative projects, others prefer to work anonymously.

6. Some donors really do have a mission statement, a personal action plan, a budget and are clear about their priorities. Most of us are not so thoroughly organized. There are pluses and minuses to even the best of plans. After all that we have said about creating a mission and a giving plan, we do recognize and honor those donors who don't want to be as organized or analytical as we propose. Whatever your style, claim it as yours while being open to what others are trying.

# Creative Ideas for Giving

Giving away money is a serious business; it should also be fun. In the course of our work all over the country, we have encountered donors who have done many creative and interesting things with their gifts. One started a retreat and writing center, another established a volunteer corps of professional associations to work with small-budget non-profits. Others established awards and memorial chairs in honor of their parents, created newsletters to keep a group of friends in touch, adopted children, and started or seeded numerous nonprofits. Here are some examples of creative givers and creative giving. We hope they stimulate your own creative thinking.

## MAKING CONNECTIONS

Michal Feder provides an example of an entrepreneurial donor and community catalyst. With lots of creativity, expertise and guidance at critical junctures, she manages her giving and leadership for her community with aplomb and radiance. But even more impressive is that her major gifts have been in the form of great ideas that have moved and sparked others' actions and mentorship.

"I want to make the world a better place," says Michal (pronounced "Michael"), now a 72-year-old retired consultant. "But I'm an entrepreneur, a starter, not a holder or maintainer of projects. Knowing that about myself has given me great freedom and clarity to make better decisions."

Michal likes making connections and getting things done. She likes tangible results, lots of people physically involved and finally, a sense of completion.

Her own assessment of the goals of some of her public service efforts is, "I look for projects where everyone benefits. I look for ideas whose time has come. I use my powers of persuasion and my abilities to make myself useful. And I hang in, within a reasonable time frame, to get the project done. That's my version of commitment!"

Here are some examples of Michal's creativity through public service activism in some of the places she has lived.

### The Foster City Library (Foster City, California)

Recognizing the need for a larger library in her community, Michal chaired a three-year effort by Foster City Friends of the Library to convince their city council to build a new facility. She then became actively involved in raising additional funds to help equip it. Michal's roles in the project ranged from catalyst and fundraiser to advocate and organizer.

### The Pocket Park (Boulder, Colorado)

Hearing that there was a plan to turn a local grassy spot in her neighborhood into a park and that local residents were bemoaning the proposed $9,000 cost, Michal pulled from her magazine pile a recent copy of the *Smithsonian* magazine with an article on parks and kids' preferences which included ideas for economical park projects. She copied the article for the association in charge of the project and lobbied the leadership at the next committee meetings for a more economical solution.

### Managing Inherited Wealth/Resourceful Women (San Francisco, California)

Michal was initially a volunteer and mentor to new members of this financial education and donor support network. She then became a board member, curriculum designer and program facilitator. At each step, she provided training for other members to pick up the thread of the work she was so instrumental in starting.

### Personal Giving

In her personal giving, Michal has instituted a number of projects, including a "fun fund." Michal recognizes that earning and managing money can sometimes be a tedious business. When she was in a position to extend some money to her three children, she wanted to introduce some perspective and levity about it. "When one can be occasionally silly, intentionally frivolous or generous with oneself, then money is in perspective. We can get a better sense of it as a useful tool and maybe not get too hung up about it," she says. For several years, Michal gave each of her children a check for $1,000 at the beginning of each year. It was theirs to spend any way they wanted. Knowing how to have fun with money for ourselves is, after all, essential if one is to know how to give to others and remain finally detached about outcome. Intention is important, but so too the journey for the gift, giver and money—each in their own fashion. The personal impact or outcome that does emerge is sometimes quite unexpected. Michal required biannual reports as a way for the family to share with each other some of the different experiences they had spending their "fun fund."

Just how much can one person do? Michal says it best. "It's not about how much money or time I give, it's about using what I have in a timely, strategic and creative way. Being entrepreneurial is part of it, but it's also about noticing opportunities, making connections and taking action."

## GROWING UP GIVING

The Jewish Fund for Justice (JFJ) is a publicly supported national foundation providing grants to organizations addressing the causes and consequences of poverty. JFJ's Youth Endowment Fund Program (YEF) gives young people a unique opportunity to become personally involved in thoughtful philanthropy, acting on the principle of *tzedakah* (justice) from an early age. Youth Endowment funds are usually established by family and friends at the time of a young person's Bat or Bar Mitzvah (age 13), with gifts of $1,000 or more, a way of accompanying their entrance into adulthood with strong support to make personal commitments to social responsibility. Monetary gifts to the fund can also mark or

honor other events, such as a birthday or school graduation.

Once a year, YEF honorees receive a ballot describing groups working with low-income youth that JFJ supports. They are encouraged to select which organizations will receive the interest earned on their individual endowment account. When an honoree turns 21, they designate their fund's principal to go either to JFJ's general fund or its Family Endowment Fund.

A newsletter written by and for YEF honorees keeps kids up to date on what's happening with the groups they've been supporting and tells them how they can get involved in social action and service projects. The newsletter introduces and connects YEF participants to each other, providing them with a forum for their ideas on social justice with peers who share their concerns about helping create a better world.

## JOINING CLIENTS IN THEIR GIVING

Eli Walker owns a small financial services firm in Minneapolis. He noticed that many of his firm's clients either don't make charitable gifts or give at a level that is below their capacity and tax advantage. To spark his clients' giving, Eli developed the "We Care Fund," through which he committed up to 8 percent of his firm's annual pre-tax profit to match his clients' giving to nonprofits in the community (the fund matches up to $50 for each new gift a client makes to a nonprofit or for each gift they make that is $50 more than a previous gift). At the end of the first year, more than 40 clients who participated in the "We Care Fund" match had made nearly 200 new gifts, for a match from the fund of nearly $10,000. Eli and his employees, clients and community realized a $20,000 nonprofit gain from the challenge/match, and everyone felt a winner. (Employees at this firm and many others can opt to have their employer match their donations to nonprofits. Check with your employer to see if your donations to nonprofits are matched.)

## INCENTIVE GIFTS

Peter Chin decided to give his children, nieces and nephews incentive gifts. For every hour they volunteered to work with a nonprofit each summer, he contributed double the number of hours, in dollars, to their college fund. For every $25 cash gift they donated or every four hours they volunteered for an organization before they turned 21, he gave each child or young adult $25 to be used for tickets to arts, theater and music events. By the time they were 21, many of the kids had been to six or eight concerts or plays that they would never have been able to afford to attend otherwise.

## GIVING COLLABORATIVELY

Giving collaboratively not only leverages individual dollars and time, it also helps reduce the sense of isolation and fear that can sometimes mark the experience of giving away money. Here are some examples from across the country of collaborative philanthropy.

### Finding a donor circle

A donor who was dedicated to international women's human rights work wanted more funding peers. She enlisted the help of the Global Fund for Women in finding other women to form a "funding circle" with her. Ten women agreed to join this circle. Each agreed to contribute $15,000 to the Global Fund for Women and to spend about eight hours a month over the next two and a half years. With a small group of staff and international activists recommended by the Global Fund, they learned about violations of female human rights around the world and decided where their pooled money should be given. There were many wonderful benefits to this arrangement: this group gave more than $100,000 to address issues concerning the human rights of women; the original donor had partners in her giving; and all the donors and activists learned a great deal about the issues as well as about working together across class, race and culture.

### Birthday Party

As part of celebrating her 50th birthday, Phoebe Valentine, a woman with inherited wealth, gave each of ten close friends a check for $5,000 to give away within the year to nonprofits of their choosing. At the end of the year, the ten friends got together to share their experience. All the donors were delighted with the exercise and Phoebe was pleased that she had multiplied her giving community and expanded her philanthropic reach. The new donors gained empathy for their philanthropist friend as they got a taste of the challenges of making choices in the face of tremendous need. They also noted that the act of giving—even someone else's money—changed the way people related to them (suddenly they were perceived with influence) and changed the way they perceived themselves (they began to want to be more involved in helping nonprofits with whatever time and money they could give).

Note: This "Birthday Party" model has been modified or replicated many times. Try giving five friends each $200 or whatever amount you choose, or jointly give away $1,000 with a group of friends on your next big birthday.

### Possibility Sundays

In early 1995, Mike and Janet Valder began a tradition they called "Possibility Sundays." First, they invited about 300 people they knew from all different aspects of their lives—politics, church, work, the neighborhood—to join them in building a new fund that would not only give money to great projects, but would help build caring community among "givers" and "receivers."

The response to their invitation was tremendous and launched what they named the Arizona Social Change Fund. To minimize administration they arranged it as a donor-advised account with the Arizona Community Foundation. In its first year and a half the fund gave away more than $37,500, with an average grant size of $5,000. Their goal is to build it up to giving $40,000–$50,000 a year.

Contributors are encouraged but not required to give a minimum of $1,000 per year; however, among the most dedicated participants are those who give far less. Everyone who contributes to the fund is invited to help direct the money. At a recent grantmaking meeting, thirty-six of the contributors met for three hours and decided by consensus on grants to three organizations. Everyone has learned by listening to each other and discerning the overall group's wisdom.

On the four months of the year that have five Sundays, the fund sponsors a Possibility Sunday event at the Valders' home. After a catered brunch there is a welcome, a prayer, and a half-hour celebration of the nonprofits being funded. The grants are awarded, and participants are invited to contribute toward the foundation's future grants to social-change organizations in the community. About a hundred people have attended each Possibility Sunday, including at least ten participants from each nonprofit showcased.

The Valders say, "The celebrations feel like 'church after church,' because they give the gathered participants a taste of the grace involved in committed social change work. When people share their deepest goals, it opens hearts. This is new to many of our friends, who had never before connected to social-change nonprofits. This fund has become one of the most meaningful projects of our lives."

### Directed Abundance

A collaborative giving program called the Flow Fund Circle began in 1991 when a woman with wealth decided to spread some of that money through people to the world. She chose twelve people whose world view and life work she respected and whose leadership and perspective she trusted.

She gave each of them $20,000 each year for three years to give away. Later, she published a booklet with a sampling of the grants they gave and some of their comments on their own experience of giving. Here are a few of those comments:

*I was surprised by the rarity of this process. In families and in friendships, you give things to each other without expectation of reward. But it's unusual to have that experience outside of intimate relationship. Being part of this was like introducing the characteristic of familial life into the wider world.*

—VIJAYUA NAGARAJAN

*This process has made me very happy. My job has been to discern what the need is and what the impact could be over the long haul. I'm most interested in what seed could be planted and how it will grow over time.*

—ANGELES ARRIEN

*This was the most innovative, cost-effective way of disbursing funds I've ever experienced. This process completely eliminates the bureaucracy…there's no cost involved in the administration, and so 100 percent of the money gets to the people are using it. There's an American Indian tradition of "the gift that moves." What I see as the brilliance of this idea is that an American funder can reach people in the most remote areas of the world, through a gift that literally passes from "warm hand to warm hand, warm heart to warm heart." There's an intimate, personal relationship at each step of the process that links us.*

—DAVID HOFFMAN

### TWO CHALLENGE GRANTS

Eve Stern got involved in philanthropy beginning in her teens as she participated in a family fund begun by her grandparents. That fund, she explains, was a pioneer in the area of challenge grants. In 1997, Eve learned that Grassroots

# *An Eclectic Collection of Giving Ideas from A to Z*

- **A**sk friends to join you in volunteering
- **B**egin a new holiday tradition: With your holiday cards to friends and family include a list of ten nonprofit organizations; ask each person to choose a group to whom you'll make a contribution in their name. Include a response card and self-addressed stamped return envelope
- **C**reate a giving pool for your family to disburse annually as a joint project
- **D**esignate charities of your choice for birthday or holiday gifts from family and friends
- **E**licit public relations and media support to leverage your personal or family foundation gifts as well as an agency's achievements
- **F**und (this will take more money)
  - an unknown playwright
  - a chair (or leadership fund) named for a teacher or activist you admire
  - your own non-profit or for-profit enterprise to achieve your own dream
  - representatives to attend conferences and meetings on your behalf
- **G**ive
  - friends checks to donate to others on your birthday
  - career or leadership training, such as an experience in Outward Bound
- **H**ire
  - staff to facilitate your own dreams
  - a public relations consultant to develop a media campaign in collaboration with staff for one of your favorite projects
- **I**nspire grantees by stipulating with your major donations that the organization have employee non-discrimination policies that protect the civil rights of all
- **J**ump to lead a fundraising campaign
- **K**eep your highest intentions and passions in sight and align your time and money appropriately
- **L**end
  - your house to an activist or nonprofit for their use for a retreat
  - your expertise to an organization
- **M**atch
  - your child's volunteer hours with financial contributions to one of their favorite organizations or causes
  - funds with other family members to make gifts larger
  - gifts of donors to a nonprofit who have never given above a certain level if they exceed that amount
- **N**etwork by telling colleagues and friends about groups you support
- **O**rganize a group of friends into a giving group, with each person contributing and jointly developing giving guidelines; periodically select organizations to which the group will donate funds
- **P**rovide an incentive for family members to give 5 percent to 20 percent of their income annually
- **Q**uery your peers about their commitments in the nonprofit sector
- **R**aise money for projects you love from people you respect
- **S**urf the Web for funding ideas and analysis (see the Resource Section)
- **T**ake a child with you to your next volunteer or service activity
- **U**nderwrite or host a party or event for a valued group or leader
- **V**alue your skills as a key influencer of peers
- **W**itness generosity by asking guests to your home to bring canned goods, clothes or other necessities in lieu of hostess gifts
- e**X**hibit leadership by giving an early lead gift to an agency's campaign
- **Y**ield more money by taking a mortgage on your house to help a local battered women's shelter buy their home
- **Z**ip through your mail with giving plan in hand

Leadership, an organization she supported, had received a $50,000 challenge grant from the Z. Smith Reynolds Foundation. In response, Eve decided to match it with a challenge grant of her own by contributing $1,000 to the organization for every contribution made by a new donor (she prefers the term "ally") under the age of 30, to a maximum of $25,000 a year for two years.

Catherine Muther, a graduate of Stanford Business School, worked for a young computer networking company. When the company went public, she benefited and decided to make a targeted gift to Stanford to improve the position and number of women faculty at the business school. She committed $100,000 and engaged the CEO of her company, also a graduate of Stanford Business School, as a giving partner. Together, they proposed a seven-figure gift for three specific uses: a Ph.D fellowship for a woman; grants for junior women faculty; and a professor-level position for a woman. Cate was clear about her objective and the strategy. Focus, partnering and leverage were key elements of success. She and her donor partner put the issue of gender equity on the table, and offered economic incentives for institutional change. Four years later, 15 percent of the faculty at Stanford Business School are women, bettering a 13 percent average for the university as a whole.

# TEN

# Money and Relationships

Whether wealthy or not, some donors want to have a more substantive role and even closer relationships with certain organizations, and decide to limit their giving to being a major donor to just one or two. People choose to work more closely with an organization for many reasons. These include wanting to work in partnership with different people to create change, take advantage of leadership opportunities, explore new careers, create a balance with a job or family, and more.

This chapter addresses becoming more involved with groups you give to by establishing clear lines of communication about the nature of your involvement, your time, and whether you want to be an anonymous donor. We also present information about extending your giving through estate planning and discuss what to consider if the question of loaning large or small amounts of money to nonprofits becomes part of your philanthropy. And finally, we provide some suggestions about how to respond to telephone solicitations and door-to-door canvassers in the context of your giving plan.

## Becoming a Partner with Organizations You Fund

If you would like to consider developing deeper relationships with the groups you support, you need to think about what you want that relationship to look like.

### COMMUNICATING DONOR INTENT

Many wonder if they should tell a nonprofit in advance if they are going to give to them or going to stop giving to them. If you give an organization $250 a year or more, we would say yes on both counts. First, if you're planning a gift, it helps development staff and directors of nonprofits with their planning and evaluation to know when a gift will be coming. Likewise, if you're certain that you will no longer be supporting a particular organization, a short note or phone call will save them from spending the resources to gain or regain your support (see "Last year of funding" letter in Appendix C).

Even more important than letting a group know that you won't be continuing your gift is to say why, especially if you've become discontent with the agency or don't agree with their direction. "This kind of honest feedback is so rare for most directors to get and it is so useful for us," said a long-time nonprofit leader. Staff are usually eager to hear how their work is perceived, to review decisions that community members, including donors, don't agree with, and to clarify misunderstandings.

### GIVING ANONYMOUSLY

Sometimes we want acknowledgment for our ideas, contributions or work on behalf of an organization. Sometimes we want to challenge other donors to put their voices and know-how where their money is. And sometimes we want people to know who we are so we can share information and leverage projects.

But at other times giving anonymously can be less complicated emotionally. No matter what the size of a gift, we may not want to be recognized as a donor among people we know or work with. Whether you choose to give anonymously is really about your own style and preference.

One situation that can arise is when you're not only a major donor, but you're also working within an organization as a staff or board member. If you don't want your role as a worker to be colored by your status as a major donor, you have a couple of options. The first is to tell the development director or executive director that you would like to keep your donations private. Explain why it's important for you and get her/him to agree to respect your anonymity and note it in your donor record.

A second option for a major gift is to have a cashier's check or a check from a donor-advised fund at a foundation, funded by you, sent to the organization. Shielded by the foundation, you're free to ask for reports or for the foundation to conduct an evaluation of your grant or gift. You are likely to pay a small fee at any institution for these services.

Any anonymous gift can have greater impact if it comes with a message. Instead of giving instructions that your gift simply be listed as anonymous to the public, consider substituting descriptions such as "from a change agent," or "from a dedicated environmentalist" or "from a concerned, gay activist."

*Over the years, I can now see that I kept giving them more money each year. But it never felt like a push. Volunteering gave me insights into their work that no proposal could ever communicate. And I wanted to be anonymous. The one person on staff who knew about my giving respected my privacy, which I really appreciated. This way, I could check out their work, quietly, help a project I cared deeply about, and know for sure how well the money was being used. While I had to deal with the internal split of being covert in my donor role, it was the best way I could maintain my boundaries and do some real good.*

—LUIS TOVAR

## ESTATE PLANNING AND PLANNED GIVING

Estate planning literally means planning for the orderly handling, disposition and administration of your goods and money when you die. There is a misconception that only those with a lot of money need to undertake thoughtful estate planning, including writing a will. That's not true. If you have any money in the bank, own a home or other real estate, or own anything of any value—from a car to a work of art—you need to decide what will happen to these things after your death. If you don't decide, the government will, and anyone you hoped would benefit will lose much of it to taxes.

The capital gains (that is the difference between an asset's purchase price and selling price when the difference is positive) on non-income-producing assets like homes, land and artwork that you may own for years or decades can be taxed at up to 80 percent when you die if those assets are not held in some sort of trust.

Estate planning lets you provide for loved ones, make gifts to causes you care about, and save your heirs income and estate taxes. In short, it lets you control where your assets will go when you die. There are many books, financial advisors and estate planners that can educate you about the specific steps in planning for your estate, be it large or small. We list some of these in the Resource Section. Here are five simple steps to consider if you haven't done any estate planning.

*1. Identify your goals*—These could include protecting assets for your beneficiaries, perpetuating a family legacy, minimizing taxes, providing for family members and making charitable gifts.

*2. Identify your beneficiaries*—As Miven Booth Trageser did (see Chapter One), spend some thoughtful time planning where and to whom you want to make these gifts. The giving plan you devised in Chapter Seven may serve as a road map.

*3. Identify your assets*—List and calculate all your assets, including cash, appreciated securities, appreciated property, tangible personal property (for example, works of art), retirement accounts and life insurance.

*4. Determine your liquidity needs*—This includes looking at the amount of money you need to live on now and projecting possible major expenses in the future, including enough money to cover expenses in case of an emergency.

*5. Create, implement and monitor a plan*—For many people this is a fun and empowering experience. Estate lawyers, tax accountants and financial planners can all help you design exactly what you want.

Charitable trust planning takes many forms and offers creative alternatives benefiting both non-charitable donors and charitable recipients. For example, charitable estate planning vehicles can allow you to transfer highly appreciated assets to a charity and still receive an income stream from those assets while you're alive. When you do this, you bypass capital gains taxes and take an income tax deduction. Or you can designate a charity as the current beneficiary of some assets (that organization receives the income) and your children as the remainder beneficiaries, so they will receive the assets following a specific period of time.

Charitable estate planning is a complex, creative and highly technical field, which a competent estate lawyer and CPA (certified public accountant) can help you with. Many people, especially those with sizable assets, find that their lawyers and tax accountants do not take the initiative to suggest charitable estate planning options. You don't need to become an expert but you do need to ask your financial advisors to further charitable trust planning vehicles that will allow you to pursue your charitable goals and you and your heirs to save substantially on taxes. There are specific vehicles, such as charitable remainder trusts, charitable lead trusts, charitable replacement trusts, pooled income funds, and charitable gift annuities. Your local university, hospital, community foundation or any other large nonprofit institution cultivating donors probably offer charitable estate planning workshops.

If you do decide that you want to leave some money or a valuable gift to a charity or nonprofit organization, the question arises as to whether you should let the organization know that they have been named as a beneficiary in your will. While knowing they will someday receive a bequest from you is important for a nonprofit organization, you should also think about the consequences of such disclosure. Will it encourage the organization to ask you for more money during your lifetime or to treat you differently than they might now as a moderate donor? Can you communicate your preference around such things while telling them about the bequest?

While you may or may not choose to let an organization know it has been named in your will, it's very important that your will be as specific as possible in a letter or on tape so that those executing your estate understand your charitable intent. Giving very specific examples of what kinds of projects or what geographic limitations you have in mind is an important part of your estate planning.

One avenue to ensuring your bequests are handled as you would wish is to designate one or more people to be charitable advisors after your death. These may be family members, friends, philanthropic or community leaders, or financial or legal professionals who have known you or your interests well. These advisors interpret your wishes with a nonprofit you may have named in a bequest or with a foundation or trust that you may have contributed to or set up upon your death. We suggest you convene this group of advisors or representatives during your lifetime, if only for one meeting, to let them know your dreams and charitable intent. Be sure the meeting has a note taker, or is taped and transcribed for use when needed.

## LOANS

Occasionally an organization faces a time-limited cash-flow bind and a short-term loan could help them get back to financial self-sufficiency. This is often true of start-up organizations or projects, or when priorities of major funders change and an organization is left without an expected source of income. Some money to tide them over while they gear up other fundraising activities may be crucial. If you've been a steady and major donor to an organization, the time might come that they approach you for a loan. If you've had a close relationship with the organization, their financial situation should not come as a surprise to you. If you're particularly close to the group, however, your emotional connection might make it more difficult to assess the practicality of their request. The Loan Analysis Worksheet on the next page presents the questions that might help you decide whether making a loan would be a good move.

# Setting Boundaries: How to Handle Requests

Most of us are not receptive when people come to our doors for money. We can't stand phone calls from groups we don't know anything about and even get cranky about calls from groups we love. We often don't want to go to lunches for donors, don't have the time to go to every event, hate direct mail. But we *do* want the country to change and know that nonprofits are part of the solution! And we know we need to be informed.

We all have preferences. Some of us love events, others find reading direct mail pieces or annual reports fascinating. The challenge is to choose to engage with the kind of fundraising that inspires us and set limits on the rest.

Here are some suggested responses that may help you establish your boundaries with requests for donations you do not wish to make.

**1. Consider the practical aspects of the loan request:**
- How much?
- How soon?
- For how long?
- Interest bearing? If yes, how much?
- Purpose?
- Chances for default?
- Provision for extension?
- Do I want collateral?
- If there is difficulty with repayment will I want to have mediation?
- Will mediation be paid for equally or by the organization?
- Will I accept a trade in lieu of cash repayment? If so, what?
- Do I want a formal contract?

**2. Consider the following questions about the organization:**
- Who's asking, do I respect and trust them?
- Leadership—who else is involved now?
- Have I checked out the situation with community or leadership sources?
- What is the organization's financial track record?
- Is this a crisis? a temporary transition?
- Is there a pattern of crisis? If so, do I want to provide support to help change the pattern?

**3. Consider the organization's overall budget and request:**
- Is the request reasonable for their need? for me?
- Do they have enough other plans for fundraising or self sufficiency efforts?
- How healthy does the agency seem to me?

| 1 | 2 | 3 | 4 | 5 |
|---|---|---|---|---|
| Thriving | | | | Brink of disaster |

- What do I think the impact of my loan will be at this time?
- Is there a way to stage the loan or make a difference with a creative solution? If so, what comes to mind?
- Am I willing to help them with other fundraising?
- What other information do I need to consider making a loan at a level that is appropriate and comfortable?
- If I make a loan, do I want to be anonymous?
- Do I want other recognition? If yes, what?

## WHEN SOMEONE COMES TO YOUR DOOR

- I'm sorry. I respect that you're trying to make a living and care about XYZ group. But I don't make gifts in this manner. If you want to leave me material, with your name on the envelope as the solicitor, I will be happy to consider it, and will call the group to check it out. If I send a contribution, I will use your envelope. Thank you.

**or:**
- I don't make gifts in this way. Don't take it personally. Good luck.

## WHEN SOMEONE CALLS FROM A GROUP YOU DON'T KNOW OR CARE ABOUT

- I'm sorry, but I don't give money over the phone. Good luck.

**or:**
- What you're doing is wonderful work, I'm sure, but I don't give in this manner. Send me some information by mail and I'll consider it.

**Other possible responses:**
- I've already allocated my budget for this year.
- I'm giving to groups that are particularly important to me.
- I'm concentrating my available funds on other issues this year.

## FOR GROUPS YOU GIVE MONEY OR TIME TO

- Please contact me only _____times a year. I would prefer to hear from you and receive information about the organization _____ (by phone, mail, personal visit?).
- Please do not pass my name on to any other organizations

**or:**

- I'm interested in what's happening in this area; please keep me informed about other organizations doing complementary work and/or events, demonstrations, or actions I might take.

## WHEN GROUPS SEND YOU MAIL YOU DON'T WANT

**Here's one donor's approach:**

- While it may take a couple of hours each year, I put all requests that I don't care about in one box, and ones I do care about in another. Then once a year, I write all the ones I don't care about and ask them to remove me from their mailing list. It's that simple. Sometimes groups buy magazine mailing lists that I may be on unbeknownst to them; so I may occasionally hear from them after all. But I feel I have done my part to try to reduce my mail and save them expenses too.

## *Inspired Philanthropists*

- Have a vision of the effect they want to have
- Do their homework and see and meet leaders and groups
- Create a giving plan and budget and give throughout the year
- Evaluate agencies and leaders they intend to invest in
- Give before they are asked
- Ask for money on behalf of organizations and leaders they support
- Bring other funders to the table
- Communicate well and are responsive to requests
- Are respectful of staff and volunteer members' time
- Offer their time and expertise as well as money
- Increase their giving annually as inflation adds to the cost of nonprofits' work
- Open doors and encourage new partnerships
- Stay committed as donors for more than three years
- Have conscious closure with organizations
- Offer their leadership on committees and boards
- Are sensitive about the inherent power differential they have as donors
- Mentor other donors
- Give both first and last in funding campaigns
- Work for lasting change by seeking the root causes of poverty and other social ills
- Never leave home without their address books

# Expanding Your Giving Horizon

*Philanthropy is commendable, but it must not cause the philanthropist to overlook the circumstances of economic injustice that make philanthropy necessary.*

—DR. MARTIN LUTHER KING, JR.

*It is not enough to be compassionate. You must act.*

— THE DALAI LAMA

## Giving Plans: Tools for a Larger Perspective

Having a giving plan is an important tool. It's one step in responding to the enormous problems that create inequality and violence and illness for millions of people every day. It's hard to conceive that your donations, whether $500 or $50,000 a year, will really make much of a dent in the vast web of those problems. Yet, through conscientious, thoughtful responses, the donations of each person contribute to positive change. Here is what some experienced donors have said:

*I know that my donations combine with thousands of others to make change and help people daily. Given my privilege, that is enough. My job is to admit my place in society's current order and to do my part to share what I can. Of hundreds of contributions I have made, fewer than 1 percent have, I think, been spent without adequate care or expertise. Trusting others to know what needs to be done and giving them the chance to do so is my task.*

. . .

*I see that the steady and intentional gifts I have made over time have built organizational stability and leadership savvy.*

. . .

*Having a giving plan has opened my eyes to what is around me and, through the choices it requires me to make, has made me more reverent of the multitude of worthy needs and more angry about the addictions and narrowness of the material world.*

. . .

*I have learned never to resist my own generous impulses.*

## Working for a Better-Functioning Democracy

*Almost anything you do will be insignificant, but it is very important that you do it.*

—MOHANDAS GANDHI

As much as Gandhi's words teach us to trust in the future effects of our actions, we're also eager to know what is reasonable to expect during our lifetimes in relationship to an issue or problem we're trying to affect. There's simply no rule of thumb. Think for a moment of how—in only a generation—attitudes about smoking, women, sexuality, the environment, violence, and parenting have changed. Behind every shift in consciousness are countless leaders, donors, organizations, and policy and public opinion makers who have shaped our thinking and changes in attitude or practice.

The project you begin or give to may not be critical to significant world change, but it may help a small community have its voice at a key moment.

Is it not the varied voices of democracy that we seek to inspire, support and bring forward when we do this work? If we are to fulfill our vision we need to expand our own perceptions of our roles and think of ourselves as full partners in change—our relationships as collaborators in the nonprofit world are very important to the health of democracy. We are part of a larger whole that includes the government, religion, families and the for-profit and nonprofit sectors. Our task is to make democracy—to make an orchestra—from the multiple voices and talents around us.

It is not enough to simply see ourselves as just small dots on the screen of giving because the great potential for change comes from our giving. But our giving has more impact and is more useful if we are part of a group or collective consciousness and can maintain our intentionality about giving and naming specific goals for changing society.

Talking with others about our goals for philanthropy and sharing our information, power and influence in decision-making with our dollars are important ways to expand the possibilities of collective power and democratic participation through philanthropy. For it is in the relationships we build and the influence we bring to leverage our efforts and knowledge that the magic of real giving lies.

## Marking the Millennium

Future historians will look back on the end of the 20th century and see many important efforts to make a global society of true compassion and altruism. They'll also see major barriers blocking the way: the technological advances of the northern countries that brought prosperity and afflu-ence to some, but left many more in need and worked to reinforce painful isolation between classes and races; the globalization of the economy that brought on the destruction of the environment, dissolution of cultures, and fragmentation of families and long-held community traditions.

Consumerism and addiction to work and money at the end of the 20th century by a small number of families in so-called developed countries has cast a shadow over a life of quality for the rest of the globe. How we live really does matter. How then shall we choose to live and how can we help others to have more choice?

On the positive side, there has been worldwide attention to shifting the trends of waste and harm caused by consumerism and capitalism and ever-shrinking natural resources. New movements supporting the economic development of those in poverty have been sparked by some banking leaders and have given rise to a proliferation of job training programs and community banks and lending programs around the world.

And a new movement in philanthropy is directing giving toward addressing some of the root causes of social problems, leading to the development of new institutions for giving, such as public charities and community foundations, with participation by those from the communities being served. In these models, wealthy people are giving communities money to give away and partnerships of activists and donors are working to make serious change. Women and people of color have also changed the face of philanthropy by demanding increased participation in giving groups, family and service clubs, and in private and corporate philanthropic programs.

As a result of this participation, by 1998, hundreds of workplace giving programs had changed their models and expanded choices from the more traditional human services agencies to environmental and civil rights groups and those supporting social change. Corporate America's giving programs are no longer just a rubber stamp for corporate marketing but a place where employee groups began to express their power by asserting their preferences for corporate support and service mandates.

Family members on the boards of private foundations moved from bowing only to the spirit of the founder or patriarch to the creation of family mission statements, pools of money for the "next generation" and student-run foundations. They developed their own community experiences through site visits and increased family member participation and, in some cases, by bringing people from outside the family onto their foundation boards to share the responsibility of giving away their money.

But the greatest sign of change at the end of the 20th century is the growing consciousness of civil society to act on its own, apart from and in some instances challenging large corporate institutions and government. Small group dialogue—from 12-step groups to community service agencies, neighborhood safety teams and local barter groups—have begun to infuse America with a new community spirit of caring. Even some members of the wealthiest top 5 percent of Americans—through the nonprofit United for a Fair Economy's Responsible Wealth program—questioned the 1997 tax reforms that gave them reduced capital gains taxes, and pledged in 1998 and beyond to support a new Fund for Fair Taxation. "Our self interest goes beyond the benefit of our own pocketbooks. If our wealth comes at the expense of programs benefitting poor communities, that is certainly not in society's whole interest," they stated.

## Creating Balance, Within and Without

*Each of us, and all of those who follow must accept this challenge of leadership—this leadership from within that unites the inner life of spirit with the outer life of service. And*

*when we do, we will discover what the great spiritual traditions have taught, and this is, simply, as we enhance our inner capacity for wholeness and freedom, we strengthen our outer capacity to love and serve. This is our common work. This is the call to the heart of philanthropy.*

—ROB LEHMAN

Those of us who are committed to personal and societal change must consider the effects of our actions on the creation of:

• true democratic, community-based participation and concern
• a national budget that is sustainable and reflects community and family needs
• a society that is educationally, economically and financially literate
• reasonable consumerism and minimal personal debt
• reduced concentration of wealth and tax benefits for the wealthy and for corporate America
• less cultural isolationism due to growing affluence and poverty
• shifts from the destruction of the environment and neighborhoods and countries due to war, poverty, and the effects of capital, to a keener awareness of the global effects of our actions
• a society that honors the sacredness of reflection, and deep, soulful listening in balance with action

As you make your donations of time and money, we urge you to:

• think big, and take small, regular actions
• act locally, nationally and internationally
• fund collaborations and statewide initiatives
• understand overarching policies and frameworks
• communicate with others about concerns, goals and intentions
• support creative leaders and cultural change communicators

- cultivate change through shifts in policy, research, the media and the arts
- give of yourself and your resources, knowing the certain guaranteed gifts of sufficiency and service
- use the infrastructure of philanthropy—all the groups and networks in our Resource Section—as your own web of learning and support
- and finally, take the long-haul approach, knowing that the small acts you do today contribute to the cumulative impact of a life spent in sharing and caring

Take time to reflect and know what you hold most sacred and what you're called to co-create. It has taken the United States more than 200 years to develop the problems that it has. People of good will working together have always challenged oppressive institutions, and change has come slowly. Sometimes change has come and gone, and come again. To think that our efforts as philanthropists are going to have any visible effect is to fail to understand the nature of the long haul, and is to demand an immediate gratification that is one of the hallmarks of class privilege, but not of social justice.

As Reinhold Neibuhr reminds us,

*Nothing worth doing can be accomplished in our lifetime; therefore we must be saved by hope. Nothing which is true or beautiful or good makes complete sense in any immediate context of history; therefore we must be saved by faith. Nothing we do, however virtuous, can be accomplished alone; therefore we must be saved by love. No virtuous act is quite as virtuous from the standpoint of friend or foe as it is from our standpoint. Therefore, we must be saved by the final favor of love, which is forgiveness.*

## SOME FINAL QUESTIONS TO REFLECT ON

1. What have you learned from your own philanthropy to date?

2. What is your dream for humanity and how do you plan to participate in its manifestation?

3. What is something you hope to change in the new century?

4. Are you moved to consider more inspired giving? What will you do?

# Appendixes and Resources

The Appendixes provide a deeper level of detail on some of the topics covered in the text and specific documents that can be helpful in being an effective donor. The final appendix, Resources, contains a sampling of organizations, Web sites and publications that can help you pursue aspects of giving that have inspired you to further research.

A.  Donor Bill of Rights
B.  The Many Ways You Can Give
C.  Sample Letters
D.  Site Visit Questions
E.  Loans to Friends
F.  Resources

# Donor Bill of Rights

Philanthropy is based on voluntary action for the common good. It is a tradition of giving and sharing that is primary to the quality of life. To assure that philanthropy merits the respect and trust of the general public, and that donors and prospective donors can have full confidence in the not-for-profit organizations and causes they are asked to support, we declare that all donors have these rights:

I    To be informed of the organization's mission, of the way the organization intends to use donated resources, and of its capacity to use donations effectively for their intended purposes.

II    To be informed of the identity of those serving on the organization's governing board and to expect the board to exercise prudent judgment in its stewardship responsibilities.

III    To have access to the organization's most recent financial statements.

IV    To be assured their gifts will be used for the purposes for which they are given.

V    To receive appropriate acknowledgment and recognition.

VI    To be assured that information about their donations is handled with respect and with confidentiality to the extent provided by law.

VII    To expect that all relationships with individuals representing organizations of interest to the donor will be professional in nature.

VIII    To be informed whether those seeking donations are volunteers, employees of the organization or hired solicitors.

IX    To have the opportunity for their names to be deleted from mailing lists that an organization may intend to share.

X    To feel free to ask questions when making a donation and to receive prompt, truthful and forthright answers.

*Developed by: American Association of Fund Raising Counsel, (AAFRC), Association for Healthcare Philanthropy (AHP), Council for Advancement and Support of Education (CASE), National Society of Fund Raising Executives (NSFRE).*

# The Many Ways You Can Give

As you can see from the brief descriptions below, there are many structured vehicles for giving. Some are more financially complex than others. You will probably want to learn a lot more about any of the ways that sound interesting to you. Increasingly, associations of nonprofits or community foundations are offering seminars on ways to give and financial planning for donors.

We urge you to meet with your local development director, community foundation staff person, planned giving specialist, lawyer or accountant to consider some of the ways you might allocate your estate or some of your income or assets during your lifetime. With just a few hours of your time and a relatively modest financial investment, you can support your goals to plan your legacy and consider your best tax and charitable advantages. After all, you can't take it with you and intentional giving and planning during your lifetime can be a wonderfully creative and clarifying process. Here are a few of the ways you can give:

**Pooled fund:** Leverage gained from a few or many individuals pooling any amount of money together. Friends, service clubs, graduation classes and, most recently, a proliferation of giving clubs have created pooled giving funds.

**Donor circle:** A group of donors who make a one- to five-year commitment to study, give and become advocates around a specific issue, region or population.

**Donor-advised fund:** A fund established by an individual donor at an existing community foundation; donors make recommendations about where they would like their contributions to go, the fund handles the administrative details.

**Private foundation:** An organization whose function is to give away money; supported by a small number of private donations.

**Family foundation:** A private foundation involving family and extended family and sometimes community advisors.

**Community foundation:** A public foundation that receives donations from a broad base and whose charter is to serve its community or issue-specific population. Community foundations vary in age, asset base, politics and level of community involvement.

**Community development financial institution (CDFI):** A lending institution (including community loan funds, community banks and credit unions) whose mission is to reinvest in targeted, underserved communities. CDFIs are supported by institutions and individual investors and donors who preserve capital while these lending agencies make it accessible to a community of organizations and individuals.

**Gifts by will:** Leaving a stated sum of money or a percentage outright to nonprofits, family, and/or friends by naming them in your will. You can also structure a trust that will benefit charitable organizations or individuals during or after your lifetime.

**Life insurance and retirement assets:** Naming nonprofits or friends as beneficiaries of at least a percentage of these assets. Financial and insurance advisors are familiar with how to do this.

**Trusts:** A variety of vehicles that can offer lifetime income and/or tax advantages to you, your family or favorite charity. Planned giving specialists and attorneys are knowledgeable about the various forms of trusts, which include charitable remainder trusts, charitable lead trusts, qualified terminable interest property, life estates, unitrusts, annuity trusts, uniform credit trusts, generation skipping trusts, and qualified personal residence trusts.

# Sample Letters

This appendix contains samples of six types of letters you may wish to send at some time to nonprofits you're involved with:

- Request for financial information
- Response to request for endowment support
- Response to request for lead gift
- Request to reduce mailings
- Notification of withdrawal of support
- Request for anonymity

**Request for Financial Information**

**LANGSTON F. CALLOWAY**
32 Greenup Avenue, #3 • Butte, MT 84569
(406) 465-8934 (phone & fax) • lcalloway@aol.com

Date

Mr. Anthony Farah
Development Director
Western Association for Historic Preservation
1245 E. 17th St., Suite 19
Helena, MT 77401

Dear Mr. Farah,

As a [current or potential] donor to your organization [or, As an interested member of the community in which your organization operates], I would like information about the administrative, program and fundraising expenses of your agency. Would you be kind enough to send me copies of your most recent 990 Forms? I understand that these records are, by law, to be made available to the public upon request. I would appreciate copies of the these documents within the next month so that I can consider the Association for my annual charitable contributions. Thank you so much for your time and attention.

Sincerely,

Langston F. Calloway

cc: Parker G. Forbes, Chair of Finance Committee

## Response to $50,000 Request for Endowment Support

**SAMANTHA ELDRIDGE**
17487 Elder Drive • Chattanooga, TN 37403
(421) 465-8934 (phone & fax) • samel@earthlink.net

Date

Ms. Cristina O'Donnell, Executive Director
The Ligeti Foundation
5396 Forest Avenue, Suite 23
Pittsburg, PA 19403

Dear Ms. O'Donnell,
After many years of supporting your organization, I was recently asked to contribute to the Legiti Foundation's endowment. In order to help me make a decision, I need to more fully understand your interest in establishing an endowment and I have some specific questions I would appreciate your answering.

• Does the foundation have a cash reserve fund of at least three months of its annual budget so that income from this endowment would not be used for operating expenses?
• For what activities do you plan to use income from the endowment?
• Do you have an investment committee that includes programmatic experts as well as financial people? people who are clear about socially responsible investments that are in alignment with the foundation's mission and programs?
• May I have a list of the members of both your board and your investment committee and a copy of the foundation's investment policies and current holdings?

Once I receive the above information, I will give the request for endowment support serious consideration. In the event that I do make the $50,000 gift, a condition of that gift will be that I receive a regular copy of the board minutes, including the financial reports.

Thank you so much for your time and attention.

Sincerely,

Samantha Eldridge

## Request for Lead Gift

**SAMANTHA ELDRIDGE**
17487 Elder Drive • Chattanooga, TN 37403
(421) 465-8934 (phone & fax) • samel@earthlink.net

Date

Mr. Robert C. Dover, Executive Director
The Brady School
5396 Forest Avenue, Suite 23
Pittsburg, PA 19403

Dear Mr. Dover,
I am writing in response to your inquiry last month into the possibility of my making a lead gift to the Brady School's "Millennium Campaign." Let me say first how honored I am to have been asked and how initially overwhelming it was to be asked to give ten times as much as I have ever given to the school. But upon reflection, I realize that if change is really going to occur, then creating and maintaining a pool of money for scholarships and to support faculty creativity is absolutely vital. So thank you for asking me. Here are some questions to which I would like your response before I send back my pledge form:

1. I would like to make a lead gift, but not be specifically public about it. It would come from the family foundation. Would that work for you?

2. How could I/we structure my gift so that it truly leverages more large donations? For example, could we make it a gift that is contingent on the campaign receiving three other gifts at $250,000 or above?

3. I am not so interested in getting tied up with the public factor of this gift as I am in the gift serving as a catalyst to others. Do you need me to put in writing why I feel so strongly about the needs for the school's growth?

I would be happy to meet privately with other donors who may be willing to consider gifts of $250,000 or more, but just don't need the public acknowledgment.

Thank you.

Samantha Eldridge

P. S. I want to be sure that my campaign gift goes to provide scholarships for minority students and money for staff. I will add this to my pledge form; this is really important to me and to the future of the school. I also want to be sure that my gift is invested in socially responsible instruments, so please send me a copy of the school's investment policies.

## Request to Reduce Mailings

**LANGSTON F. CALLOWAY**
32 Greenup Avenue, #3 • Butte, MT 84569
(406) 465-8934 (phone & fax) • lcalloway@aol.com

Date

Mr. Zev Mendel, Development Director
Mt. Zion Hospital Foundation
8925 Clarinda Street, Room 234
Los Angeles, CA 90047

Dear Mr. Mendel,

I hope you can help me solve a problem. I am concerned about the amount of mail that I receive from your organization, among others. As an environmentalist, I would like to request the following: I would like to be moved from your regular mailing list to an anonymous donor or "special services" list. If I am contacted only once a year, either through a mailing or with an in-person visit, which may include the mailing of one letter and a copy of your annual report, then I will feel that I am being adequately updated about the foundation's work. If you can fulfill this request, I pledge to send the foundation a minimum of $1,000/year for three years within sixty (60) days of receiving the annual report or the one annual mailing. If after three months I am still receiving regular mailings from the foundation, then I will assume that you are not able to grant my request and I will withdraw my pledge. Thank you very much.

Langston F. Calloway

P. S. Please continue to list me in your donor list by name. If the list is by amount, then simply list me as anonymous, or "a loving former patient."

cc: Barbara Rossman, President, Board of Trustees

## Notification of Withdrawal of Support

**SAMANTHA ELDRIDGE**
17487 Elder Drive • Chattanooga, TN 37403
(421) 465-8934 (phone & fax) • samel@earthlink.net

Date

Mr. Andrew W. Vaughn
Development Director
The Martin and Lila Harrison Trust
245 E. 72nd Street, Suite 547
New York, New York 10021

Dear Mr. Vaughn,

I have been a donor to the Trust for the last six years. And while I greatly value the important work you do, the priorities for my giving have changed and I feel that a seven-year commitment is the maximum that I want to make to most organizations. As a result, the enclosed contribution of $ _____ will be my last to the Trust. During the next six months, I will be happy to work with you to identify and solicit a donor who can replace my gift. Please give me a call or write me in February so we can talk about this in more detail.

Sincerely,

Samantha Eldridge

cc: Khiem Thi Truong, Executive Director

**Request for Anonymity**

**LANGSTON F. CALLOWAY**
32 Greenup Avenue, #3 • Butte, MT 84569
(406) 465-8934 (phone & fax) • lcalloway@aol.com

Date

Ms. Joan C. Chin, Development Director
Asian American Lawyers for the Arts
1736 W. Magnuson Street, Suite 212
Minneapolis, MN 46742

Dear Ms. Chin,

I understand that you have just joined AALA as the new develop-ment director. It's a wonderful organization, and one that I enthusi-astically support. Although I'm sure you've been briefed about the major donors to the organization, I would just like to make sure that you understand the conditions for my continued support. I am an anonymous donor. What this means for me is that I:

- do not wish to be listed by name in any publications or lists, unless it is under an "anonymous" category

- am happy to receive mailings, but do not want to be solicited by anyone other than you or the executive director

- do not want my donor history printed out and included in any com-mittee meeting or board discussions

- do not want to be called for any reason, including invitations to events, requests to volunteer, except by you or the executive director

- do not want my name discussed with any other staff or board mem-ber, or with any other nonprofit director or staff, even in passing.

(over)

My anonymity is important to me. I've worked very consciously to create my privacy and I have every expectation that you will respect and help me maintain it. If you would like to talk with me about this further, please don't hesitate. I realize that AALA may not have many anonymous donors who desire this level of detail. So if you have questions, I will do whatever I can to help you fully understand my request and its implications.

Thank you so much for your time.

Sincerely,


Langston F. Calloway


P.S. Please keep this letter permanently in your file.

# Site Visit Questions

## PREPARATION

1. Define the goal of your site visit, such as to learn about the organization and its work, or to determine the appropriateness of a future or further gift.

2. Read the proposal or background information.

3. Think about your expectations, questions and concerns in advance.

## QUESTIONS TO ASK

### Program and Leadership

1. What is the organization's mission or primary purpose?

2. What are the organization's primary programs or activities and their immediate and long-range purposes?

3. What is the organization's primary strategy to achieve those goals?

4. What is the most exciting thing the group is doing now?

5. How does your community perceive the organization's work?

### History

6. How long has the organization been doing what it does? Why was it formed? Has its mission or purpose changed during the past three to five years?

7. What is the organization's vision for its work over the next year? Three years? Do you have a written and approved strategic plan? If so, may I have a copy? How and why do you see the work changing? What impact do you think your project has had on the issue the organization is addressing?

8. Who does your organization serve? Who are your constituencies?

9. Who is your leadership body? What kind of people and talent have been involved? How do you support your staff and board to develop their skills and awareness?

### Organizational Functioning

10. How many people work with and for the organization, in what capacities? Do board members, senior staff and volunteers reflect your clients and other constituents?

11. Who decides what? Are constituents involved in staff, board and volunteer leadership?

12. How does your organization define success? How do you decide when to alter strategy or direction?

13. Is there anything else you'd like me to know?

### Fundraising

14. What is your budget?

15. How much is earned, how much is contributed?

16. What are the organization's sources of earned and contributed income?

17. What are your fundraising goals? Do you have a fundraising plan? Who is involved in fundraising?

18. Does the organization have a cash reserve? How big is it as a proportion of the budget?

19. Does the organization have an endowment? How large is it? What is its purpose?

20. If I am unable to fund this project how will this affect its going forward?

21. What is the most useful gift a donor or foundation could give you now?

# Loans to Friends

What would you do if you heard that someone who had been a close friend in high school had been diagnosed with cancer, was a single mom, and was down and out?

Here are some responses we've heard:

- Do nothing. If she called me to ask for help, then I could consider responding, but it would depend on whether it was a current relationship for me. No need to rescue when not invited to do so.
- I would immediately send her, anonymously, $5,000. No questions asked.
- I might check around and ask more about her situation from those who were more recently close to her, call her, talk and get information about what she said she needed, and then consider based on all that what to do. If she needed financial support, I might ask her about her options, and failing any, give some money but, better yet, I might organize a letter to our high school class and ask everyone to chip in.
- I would go check out what she needed. Often hands-on stuff, like helping with the kids or phone calls or bureaucratic red tape (like filling out all those terrible insurance and hospital forms) is just as helpful as sending a check and I'd be more comfortable supporting these kinds of things.

Being a giver presents new opportunities for both connection with others and isolation, for opening your heart and mind to the inequities around you, or numbing your sense of compassion with guilt for having too much and fear of being exploited. You can help make real change that is meaningful to you and others, that respects your sense of self as well as that of others, or you can become entangled in other people's problems, violating your own boundaries as well as theirs, and ultimately being effective for no one. Establishing your own boundaries, knowing your financial capacities, setting your goals, and developing your own budget or decision-making process before you're confronted with difficult decisions—all these steps help.

- I have one category in my budget, called "life's dilemmas" and another called "donor's whim." These give me permission to engage in real life's happenings, but also give me some boundaries for my own protection and self-respect.
- I feel a responsibility to learn to lend money to friends and nonprofits. The banks aren't doing it for even good people. I see it as part of my responsibility as a monied person, and I've come to enjoy it. Lots of people have been helped and 98 percent of the loans have been trouble-free, and have even deepened my trust with my friends.
- I had the best of intentions when I loaned my friends money, but in almost every case, something went wrong. I can now see my own part in not sitting down and talking about expectations, about mutual goals for the loans, about possible consequences, and asking my friends how we might jointly handle communication and problem solving if they were not able to pay back the loans on time. I still feel that loaning money to people who need it is key, but I've decided to lend it to community loan funds to eliminate some of the personal complexities; I just wasn't ready to do all the negotiating and partnership required. (See Resource Section for more information on community development

loan funds and microenterprise development funds.)

If you're going to make a loan, recognize that it is a business transaction and will be most successful if handled in a friendly but businesslike manner, which means written agreements about payback schedules and interest, if any. If this is uncomfortable for you, you might rather just give an outright gift. If you're decidedly opposed to giving loans, be sure you have a global statement that lets people know that. Saying, "I'm sorry, I make it a policy not to loan money to friends," assures the person asking that this is not a personal rejection.

When considering a loan to a friend, the first several questions presented in the Loan Analysis Worksheet for use with loans to organizations (see page 75) will be helpful. In addition, there are some emotional aspects to loaning money to friends that may not be present in loans to organizations. You might consider the following emotional features that come into play. Place an X at the point along each continuum you feel would best represent the impact of the transaction.

## ADDITIONAL QUESTIONS CONCERNING LOANS TO FRIENDS

**I am**
  happy to help_____ feel obligated

**Our relationship will**
  be strengthened_____ weakened

**I will feel I am**
  affirming _____ rescuing

**I will feel**
  comfortable_____ ambivalent

**I will feel**
  useful_____ used

# Resources

Much of the information in this resource list is excerpted from *Welcome to Philanthropy: Resources for Individuals and Families Exploring Social Change Giving* by Christopher Mogil and Anne Slepian, available from National Network of Grantmakers.

## Creating a Giving Plan

### BOOKS AND ARTICLES

Ram Dass and Paul Gorman, *How Can I Help? Stories and Reflections on Service*. New York: Alfred Knopf, 1985.

Steve Paprocki, "The Why and How of Personal Giving Plans," in *Grassroots Fundraising Journal*. August and October, 1986. Chardon Press, P.O. Box 11607, Berkeley, CA 94712. Phone: 510/704-8714; fax: 510/649-7913; Web site: www.chardonpress.com.

### INTERNET RESOURCES

BENEFICE (www.benefice.com) A Web site that provides a step-by-step process for developing a personal giving plan, including resource listings to national nonprofits. E-mail: benefice @benefice.com 800/711-0102.

Chardon Press (www.chardonpress.com.) Download an *Inspired Philanthropy* sample giving plan and order other philanthropy- and fundraising-related books and journals from this, our publisher's Web site.

## Effective and Strategic Giving

### BOOKS

Chuck Collins and Pam Rogers, *Robin Hood Was Right*, 2nd edition, forthcoming. Funding Exchange, 666 Broadway, #500, New York, NY 10012. Phone: 212/529-5300.

Ellen Furnari, Carol Mollner, Teresa Odendahl, and Aileen Shaw, *Exemplary Grantmaking Practices Manual*. 1997. National Network of Grantmakers, 1717 Kettner Blvd., Suite 110, San Diego, CA 92101. Phone: 619/231-1348; E-mail: nng@nng.org.

*Giving USA*, American Association of Fund Raising Counsel Trust for Philanthropy. AAFRC, 25 W. 23d Street, New York, NY 10036. Phone: 212/354-5799.

Douglas M. Lawson, *Give to Live: How Giving Can Change Your Life*. Poway, CA: ALTI Publishing, 1991.

_____. *Volunteering*. Poway, CA: ALTI Publishing, 1998.

John Levy, *Is it Better to Give than to Receive?* (booklet) Available free from: 842 Autumn Lane, Mill Valley, CA 94941. Phone: 415/383-3951.

Christopher Mogil and Anne Slepian, *We Gave Away a Fortune*, Available from: Impact Project—2244 Alder Street, Eugene, OR 97405. Phone: 541/343-2420; E-mail: impact@efn.org. Web site: www.efn.org/~impact.

Christopher Mogil and Anne Slepian, *Welcome to Philanthropy: Resources for Individuals and Families Exploring Social Change Giving*. 1997. National Network of Grantmakers, 1717 Kettner Blvd., Suite 110, San Diego, CA 92101. Phone: 619/231-1348; E-mail: nng@nng.org. Web site: www.nng.org.

Frances Moore-Lappé and Paul Martin Du Bois, *The Quickening of America: Rebuilding Our Nation, Remaking Lives*. San Francisco: Jossey-Bass, 1994.

Teresa Odendahl, *Charity Begins at Home: Generosity & Self-Interest Among the Philanthropic Elite*. New York: Basic Books, 1990.

Susan A. Ostrander, *Money for Change: Social Movement Philanthropy at the Haymarket People's Fund*. Philadelphia: Temple University Press, 1995.

Claude Rosenberg, Jr., *Wealthy and Wise: How You and America Can Get the Most of Your Giving*. Boston: Little, Brown & Co.,1994.

Aileen Shaw, *Preserving the Public Trust: A Study of Exemplary Practices in Grantmaking*. 1997. National Network of Grantmakers, 1717 Kettner Blvd., Suite 110, San Diego, CA 92101. Phone: 619/231-1348; E-mail: nng@nng.org.

Sondra C. Shaw and Martha A. Taylor, *Reinventing Fundraising: Realizing the Potential of Women's Philanthropy*. San Francisco: Jossey-Bass, 1995.

## NEWSLETTERS

"Family Philanthropy," in *Family Money: A commentary on the Unspoken Issues Related to Wealth*, Winter 1996. JGB Associates, 1515 4th Street, Suite B, Napa, CA 94559. Phone: 707/255-6254.

*Initiatives: A Newsletter on Strategic Philanthropy*. The Philanthropic Initiative, 77 Franklin Street, Boston, MA 02110. Phone: 617/338-2590; E-mail get2us@TPI.org; Web site: www.tpi.org.

"What Makes Giving Satisfying?" (issue #2), "Creative Giving: Stepping Beyond the Norm"(issue #12), and "Family Foundations" (issue #16) of *More Than Money* (quarterly journal). Subscriptions: $35 a year for individuals, $75 for organizations. Back issues: $7 to non-members. Impact Project, 2244 Alder Street, Eugene, OR 94705. Phone: 541/343-2420; Web site: www.efn.org/~impact.

*Responsive Philanthropy* (quarterly journal). National Committee for Responsive Philanthropy, 2001 S Street, NW, Suite 620, Washington, D.C. 20009. Phone: 202/387-9177; Web site: www.ncrp.org.

*Too Much*, a quarterly commentary on Capping Excessive Income and Wealth. Council on International and Public Affairs (CIPA) and United for a Fair Economy. Contact: CIPA, 777 United Nations Plaza, Suite 3C, New York, NY 10017. Phone: 212/972-9877.

*Women's Philanthropy Institute News*, Women's Philanthropy Institute, 1605 Monroe Street, Suite 105, Madison, WI 53711-2052. Phone: 608/286-0980; E-mail: andrea@women-philanthropy.org. Web site: www.women-philanthropy.org.

## PHILANTHROPIC CONSULTING FIRMS

Class Action, 245 Main Street #207, Northampton, MA 01060. Phone: 413/585-9709; E-mail: jladd@igc.org.

Community Consulting Services, P.O. Box 428, Ross, CA 94957. 415/461-5539; E-mail: tracygary1@aol.com.

Grants Management Associates, Inc., 230 Congress Street, Boston, MA 02110. Phone: 617/426-7172. Fax: 617/426-5441; E-mail: grantman@igc.apc.org.

Hubbell Associates, 283 Second Street East, Sonoma, CA 94576. Phone: 707/938-8248.

National Center for Family Philanthropy, 1220 19th Street, NW, Suite 804, Washington, D.C. 20036. Phone: 202/293-3423.

Ottinger and Careth Foundations (Meg Gage and Katrin Verclass), 250 N. Pleasant Street, Suite 2, Amherst, MA 01002. Phone: 413/256-0349.

PDM Associates, 76 Wellwood Road, Portland, ME 04103. Phone: 207/772-3246; E-mail: pdmalcolm@aol.com.

The Philanthropic Collaborative, Inc., Room 5600, 30 Rockefeller Plaza, New York, NY 10112. Phone: 212/649-3424.

The Philanthropic Initiative, 77 Franklin Street, Boston, MA 02110. Phone: 617/338-2590; E-mail: get2us@tpi.org; Web site: www.tpi.org.

Philanthropic Strategies, 1730 M Street NW, Suite 404, Washington, D.C. 20036. Phone: 202/338-8055.

The Philanthropy Group, E-mail: lwgruber@aol.com; cahayes179@aol.com; lmgreen@eathlink.net.

Strategic Philanthropy, Australia, 165 Flinders Street, Melbourne VIC 3000; Phone: 03/650-4400; E-mail: lance@creativeaccess.com.au.

Strategic Philanthropy, International, P.O. Box 428, Ross, CA 94957. Phone: 415/461-5539; E-mail: tracygary1@aol.com.

## ORGANIZATIONS

**Ma'yan**—Conducts workshops for Jewish women on service and philanthropy. Contact: Ma'yan c/o JCC, 15 W. 65th Street, 8th Floor, New York, NY 10023. Phone: 212/580-0099.

**Ministry of Money**—Offers programs exploring money, wealth and meaning from a Christian perspective. Weekend workshops, including a special women's program, trips to Third World countries, and a bi-monthly newsletter. Contact: 2 Professional Drive, Suite 220, Gaithersburg, MD 20879. Phone: 301/670-9606; E-mail: minmon@erols.com.

**National Committee on Planned Giving**—Conducts research, offers publications, workshops and conferences. Contact: NCPG, 233 McCrea St., Suite 400, Indianapolis, IN 46225-1030. Phone: 317/269-6274; E-mail: ncpg@zupui.edu. Web site: www.ncpg.org.

**National Society of Fundraising Executives**—Offers many workshops, conferences and publications. 1101 King Street, Suite 700, Alexandria, Virginia 22314-2967; Phone: 800/666-FUND, 703/684-0410; E-mail: nsfre@nsfre.org. Web site: www.nsfre.org.

**The Gill Foundation Outgiving Project**—Seeks to increase the overall funding base for organizations serving the lesbian, gay, bisexual and transgendered communities; offers donors resources to enhance their giving, including conferences for those giving $10,000 or more to gay and lesbian projects. Contact: Mickey MacIntyre, 1225 Eye Street, NW, Suite 930, Washington, D.C. 20005. Phone: 202/898-6340; fax: 202/898-6341; E-mail: outgiving@gillfoundation.org. Web site: www.gillfoundation.org.

**The Philanthropy Workshop**—Offers a ten-month course for individuals or families with significant wealth who are interested in developing strategic plans for their own philanthropy or for their family foundation. Contact: Rockefeller Foundation, 420 Fifth Avenue, New York, NY 10018-2702. Phone: 212/869-8500.

# Where to Give: Resources & Starting Points

## ORGANIZATIONS

*The organizations listed here are public foundations and national associations. They can direct you to nonprofit groups to give (or lend) to or to volunteer with, or you can give directly to these groups. These foundations are community-based resources whose staff and volunteer committees assess nonprofit groups and organize funding for them. Their annual reports and newsletters describe groups that receive grants. You can also ask for more comprehensive documents (called dockets) that list and evaluate projects and groups the foundation is interested in.*

**Astraea National Lesbian Action Foundation**—Provides economic and social support to projects that actively work to eliminate those forms of oppression based on race, age, sex, economic exploitation, physical and mental ability, anti-Semitism and all other factors that affect lesbians and gay men. Contact: 116 East 16th Street, 7th Floor, New York, NY 10003. Phone: 212/529-8021; E-mail: anlaf@aol.com; Web site: www.astraea.org.

**A Territory Resource (ATR)**—Provides funding and technical assistance to grassroots groups in the Northwest United States. Organizers and donors set funding priorities together, conduct site visits and discuss which projects to recommend for funding. Programs include managing money conferences, panels and workshops on various social justice issues, wealth affinity groups and donor-advised accounts. Contact: 603 Stewart Street, Suite 1007, Seattle, WA 98101. Phone: 206/624-4081; E-mail: atrgrants.aol.com; Web site: www.atrfoundation.org.

**Council on Foundations**—Provides substantial national support services for different sectors of philanthropy, including family foundations. Offers conferences, many practical reference publications, and information about philanthropic affinity groups, family foundations and regional associations of grantmakers. Contact: 1828 L Street NW, #300, Washington, D.C. 20036. Phone: 202/466-6512; Web site: www.cof.org.

**Funding Exchange**—A national network of alternative foundations that supports progressive grassroots organizing locally and nationally. Community activists play a central role as decisionmakers in the grant-making process. Three national grantmaking programs and 15 local funds operate in 24 states. The Funding Exchange network gives $3–5 million per year to grassroots social justice organizations nationwide. Offers educational programs for people with inherited wealth, donor-advised grantmaking services and an international working group. Contact: 666 Broadway, #500, New York, NY 10012. Phone: 212/529-5300; E-mail: fexexc@aol.com. Web site: www.fex.org.

*Member Funds of the Funding Exchange:*

**Appalachia.** Appalachian Community Fund, 517 Union Avenue, #206 Knoxville, TN 37902. Phone: 423/523-5783.

**California (Los Angeles).** Liberty Hill, 1316 Third Street Promenade, #B-4, Santa Monica, CA 90401. Phone: 310/458-1450.

**California (Northern).** Vanguard Public Foundation, 383 Rhode Island Street, #301, San Francisco, CA 94103. Phone: 415/487-2111.

**California (Santa Barbara).** Fund for Santa Barbara, 735 State Street, Suite 211, Santa Barbara, CA 93101. Phone: 805/962-9164.

**Colorado.** Chinook Fund, 2418 W. 32nd Avenue, Denver, CO 80211. Phone: 303/455-6905.

**Georgia/North Carolina/South Carolina.** Fund for Southern Communities, 547 Ponce De Leon Avenue, #100, Atlanta, GA 30308. Phone: 404/876-4147.

**Hawai'i.** The People's Fund, 1325 Nuuanu Avenue, Honolulu, HI 96817. Phone: 808/526-2441.

**Illinois (Chicago).** Crossroads Fund, 3411 West Diversey Avenue, #20, Chicago, IL 60647. Phone: 773/227-7676.

**Minneapolis.** Headwaters Fund, 122 W. Franklin Avenue, Minneapolis, MN 55404. Phone: 612/879-0602.

**New England.** Haymarket People's Fund, 42 Seaverns Avenue, Boston, MA 02130. Phone: 617/522-7676.

**New York.** North Star Fund, 305 7th Avenue, Fifth Floor, New York, NY 10001-6008. Phone: 212/620-9110.

**Oregon.** McKenzie River Gathering Foundation, 3558 SE Hawthorne, Portland, OR 97214. Phone: 503/233-0271. *Eugene office:* 454 Willamette St., Eugene, OR 97401. Phone: 541/485-2790.

**Pennsylvania (greater Philadelphia) and Camden, NJ.** Bread and Roses Community Fund, 1500 Walnut Street, #1305, Philadelphia, PA 19102. Phone: 215/731-1107.

**Pennsylvania (SW Pennsylvania).** Three Rivers Fund, 100 N. Braddock Avenue, #207, Pittsburgh, PA 15208. Phone: 412/243-9250.

**Wisconsin.** Wisconsin Community Fund, 122 State Street, #508, Madison, WI 53703. Phone: 608/251-6834.

**Global Fund for Women**—Funds grassroots women's groups around the world on issues of leadership, poverty and economic autonomy, reproductive freedom, the rights of sexual minorities and the prevention of violence against women. Contact: 425 Sherman Avenue, Suite 300, Palo Alto, CA 94306. Phone: 650/853-8305; E-mail: gfw@globalfundforwomen.org; Web site: www.globalfundforwomen.org.

**Jewish Fund For Justice**—Makes grants to grassroots organizations working to combat poverty and seeks to bring a Jewish presence to interfaith actions for social change. Contact: 260 5th Avenue, Suite 701, New York, NY 10001. Phone: 212/213-2113; E-mail: JusticeUSA@aol.com.

**Ms. Foundation For Women**—Supports the efforts of women and girls to govern their lives and influence the world around them. Directs resources to break down barriers faced by women of color, low-income women, older women, lesbians, and women with disabilities. Contact: 120 Wall Street, 33d Floor, New York, NY 10005. Phone: 212/742-2300; E-mail: info@ms.foundation.org; Web site: www.ms.foundation.org.

**National Alliance for Choice in Giving**—An association of innovative cooperative fundraising organizations. Provides resources, training, and national support to enhance the ability of local and statewide federations to participate in workplace fundraising campaigns and to provide interested employees and employers with the opportunity to contribute their skills, time and resources to building a stronger and healthier community. Works with 53 federations covering 32 states. They can provide you with information about the alternative federation near you. Contact: 2001 O Street, NW, Washington, D.C. 20036. Phone: 202/296-8470; E-mail: 74041.2454.

**National Black United Funds**—Seeks to promote expansion of African-American philanthropy nationwide by obtaining access to employee charitable giving campaigns, conducting training institutes and conferences and supporting self-help initiatives identified as community priorities. 20 affiliates, 12 local federations, and a Natinal Black United Federation of Charities with 48 affiliates. Contact: 40 Clinton Street, Newark, NJ 07102. Phone: 210/643-5122; Web site: www.nbuf.org.

**National Community Capital Association**—Represents 49 member community development financial institutions (CDFIs) that provide capital, training and other services for community-based development projects in low-income urban, rural, and reservation-based communities throughout the United States. Offers a range of capacity-building, performance-based financing and public policy programs. Contact: 924 Cherry Street, 2nd Floor, Philadelphia, PA 19107-2411. Phone: 215/923-4754; Web site: www.communitycapital.org.

**National Network of Grantmakers**—A membership organization of progressive funders: individual donors, trustees, board members and employees of grantmaking and workplace fundraising programs. Works primarily within organized philanthropy to increase financial and other resources to groups committed to economic and social justice. Publishes *The Grantmakers Directory*, which includes NNG's Common Grant Appication, and organizes a national conference and other forums for working with colleagues to promote a progressive agenda within philanthropy. Contact: 1717 Kettner Blvd. Suite#110, San Diego, CA 92101. Phone: 619/231-1348; E-mail: nng@nng.org. Web site: www.nng.org.

**Peace Development Fund**—Provides financial assistance, training and technical support to social and environmental justice organizations. Offers programs that assist donors to become more educated and effective and to build collaborative projects between funders and other organizations. Contact: Box 1280, Amherst, MA 01004. Phone: 413/256-8306; E-mail: pdf@javanet.com.

**RESIST**—Funds small-budget groups that struggle towards a broad vision of social justice while continuing to oppose political and institutional oppression. Publishes a newsletter that focuses on topics of interest to progressive activists and the pamphlet, "Finding Funding: A Beginner's Guide to Foundation Research." Contact: 259 Elm Street, Suite 201, Somerville, MA 02144. Phone: 617/623-5110; E-mail: resistinc@igc.org. Web site: www.resistinc.org.

**San Diego Foundation for Change**—Provides community organizing funding in the San Diego area for progressive social change in the areas of racial equality, economic justice, civil liberties, and environmental justice. Contact: 1717 Kettner Blvd. Suite 100, San Diego, CA 92101. Phone: 619/235-4647.

**The Shefa Fund**—Provides expertise, advice and grantmaking services nationally to Jewish funders. Links Jewish values and ethics with the use of financial resources for social justice and spiritual innovation. Newsletter, annual report and several publications include *Jews, Money and Social Responsibility*, which discusses socially responsible shopping, investment and philanthropy from a progressive Jewish perspective. Contact: 805 East Willow Grove Avenue, Suite 2D, Wyndmoor, PA 19038. Phone: 215/247-9704; E-mail: shefafnd@libertynet.org.

**Third Wave Foundation**—A national activist philanthropic organization for young women between the ages of 15 and 30. Informs, networks and empowers a generation of young feminist activists through technical assistance, public education campaigns and grantmaking for young women (ages 13-30); run by women and men under the age of 35. Produces a conference and listserve for young people with substantial earned or inherited wealth. Contact: 116 E. 16th Street, 7th floor, New York, NY 10003. Phone: 212/388-1898; Web site: www.feminist.com/3wave.htm.

**Tides Foundation**—Promotes social justice, economic opportunity, a more robust democratic process, and sustainable environmental practices through its grant-making program. Enables individuals to set up donor-advised funds, and provides a range of program and administrative services. Contact: Box 29903, San Francisco, CA 94129. Phone: 415/561-6400; E-mail: tides@igc.org.

**United Ways of America**—Approximately 1,300 community-based United Way organizations that, through a single campaign, raise funds to support local agency service providers in the areas of health and human-care services. Contact: 701 N. Fairfax Street, Alexandria, VA 22314-2045. Phone: 703/836-7100 or 800/411-UWAY; Web site: www.unitedway.org.

**Women's Funding Network**—Brings together more than 90 public and private women's foundations and individual donors to promote the development and growth of funds that empower women and girls. Some local women's funds offer conferences for women of varying financial means to increase their financial literacy, including workshops on financial planning, socially responsible investing, funding and women's economic development. Contact: 332 Minnesota Street, Suite E-840, St. Paul, MN 55101. Phone: 612/227-1911; E-mail: wfn@wfnet.org; Web site: www.wfnet.org.

**Working Group on Funding Lesbian and Gay Issues**—Advocates for increased support of gay, lesbian, bisexual and transgendered issues within organized philanthropy. Provides an information center for individual and organizational grantmakers and grantseekers, a national directory of funders who support LGBT projects and programs, a guide for grantmakers, presentations, and local and regional seminars. Contact: 116 E. 16th Street, 7th Floor, New York, NY 10003. Phone: 212/475-2930.

## BOOKS AND PUBLICATIONS

*American Benefactor Magazine*, 575 Lexington Ave., 35th Floor, New York, NY 10022. Phone: 800/818-0724 (NY only); 212/223-3100.

Robert Graham, *Fifty/Fifty at Fifty*. 1997. Pacific Rim Publishers. P.O. Box 1776, Carmel, CA, 93921. Phone: 888/361-4667.

Jeffrey Hollender, *How to Make the World a Better Place: A Guide to Doing Good*. New York: Norton, 1995.

Lewis Hyde, *The Gift: Imagination and the Erotic Life of Property*. New York: Vintage, 1983.

*The Independent Sector Publications Catalogue: Materials for Today's Leaders in Voluntary Action*. Independent Sector. P.O. Box 343, Waldorf, MD 20604. Phone: 301/490-3229; Web site: www.indepsec.org.

Genevieve Vaughan, *For-Giving: A Feminist Criticism of Exchange*. 1997. Available from: Plain View Press, P.O. Box 33311, Austin, TX 78764. Phone: 512/441-2452.

## NON-PROFIT RATING ORGANIZATIONS

*The following organizations will be able to tell you about large and well-established charities. Most grassroots organizations will not be listed here.*

**American Institute of Philanthropy**—Publishes *Charity Rating Guide & Watchdog Report*. Evaluates and grades organizations according to percent of revenues spent on charitable programs, cost to raise $100, and years of available assets. Contact: 4905 DelRay Avenue, #300, Bethesda, MD 20814. Phone: 301/913-5200.

**Council of Better Business Bureau's Philanthropic Advisory Service**— Sets standards for charitable solicitations and collects information on charitable organizations in the U.S. that solicit nationally. An index to these reports is on the Web page, with information on whether a particular organization meets their standards and how to obtain the complete report (free of charge) by regular mail. Contact: 4200 Wilson Blvd., Suite 800, Arlington, VA 22203-1804. Phone: 703/276-0100; Web site: www.bbb.org/cbbb.pas.html.

**Guidestar Directory of American Charities**—Publishes reports on nonprofit organizations, including information on financial ratios and indicators in the areas of program, fundraising, contribution and grants, debt and savings. Contact: 1126 Professional Drive, Williamsburg, VA 23185. Phone: 757/229-4631; Web site: www.guidestar.org.

**National Charities Information Bureau**—Rates organizations according to criteria relating to board governance, organizational purpose, consistency of programs, accurate promotional information, financial support and related activities, use of funds, annual reporting and accountability. Offers free booklet, *Wise Giving Guide*. Contact: 19 Union Square West, New York, NY 10003. Phone: 212/929-6300; Web site: www.give.org/.

## INTERNET RESOURCES
**Commit More than Charity (www.commit98.net)**—Free giving guides for San Francisco, Seattle and Portland; program and financial information on community organizations.

**Foundation Center (www.fndcenter.org)**—Listing of all foundation center libraries and their resources, including the largest collection of foundation annual reports.

**Giving Discussion List**—E-mail discussion list address: giving@envirolink.org (to link). To subscribe, E-mail: listproc@envirolink.org. Use "subscribe giving" in message body. Contact: Cliff Lindesman, list owner; E-mail: clandesm@panix.com.

**Independent Sector (www.indepsec.org)**—Information and statistics to support and encourage philanthropy, volunteerism and nonprofit initiatives by a coalition of foundation, corporate and volunteer-based organizations.

**International Donor Dialogue (www.internationaldonors.org)**— A resource and forum about international giving.

**Leave A Legacy (www.leavealegacy.org)**—Planned giving information and support.

**The Idea List; Contact Center Network (www.contact.org)**— Contains a directory of resources on the Web and links to more than 5,000 nonprofit organizations.

**The Internet Nonprofit Center (www.nonprofits.org).**

**The Meta-Index of Nonprofit Organizations on the Web (www.philanthropy-journal.org.)**—Nonprofit internet resources sprinkled with philanthropy-related links.

**The Support Center (www.supportcenter.org/sf/)**—Includes the center's workshop catalogue and access to frequently asked questions on a range of fundraising topics.

# Money

## DONOR SUPPORT AND ACTIVISM
**Comfort Zone**—Encourages young adults with wealth to take charge of their money, connect to their peers, and support social change. Provides accessible information on the personal, technical, political and philanthropic aspects of wealth to people in their 20s, primarily through distribution of the resource guide, *Money Talks. So Can We.* Contact: P.O. Box 336, North Cambridge, MA 02140. Phone: 617/441-5567.

**Donor Organizers' Network**—A program area of the National Network of Grantmakers. Aims to serve and expand the number of people and organizations helping individuals with inherited and earned wealth to become partners in progressive social change through increased giving, volunteerism, socially responsible investing and activism. Offers regional and national conferences, study groups and other programs that encourage communication, collaboration, and mutual learning among its members. Contact: 1717 Kettner Blvd. Suite #110, San Diego, CA 92101. Phone: 619/231-1348.

**Impact Project**—Assists people with financial abundance (inherited or earned) to realize their life goals and engage their money, energy, and talents towards creating a more just, sustainable, and joyful world. Offers workshops, individual money counseling, and literature. Also works to organize the field of donor organizing. Quarterly journal, *More than Money*, explores the meaning of money with personal stories, articles, and humor. Subscription: $35 a year. Contact: 2244 Alder Street, Eugene, OR 97405. Phone: 541/343-2420; E-mail: impact@efn.org. Web site: www.efn.org/~impact.

**Jewish Funders Network**—Networking and education for foundation trustees and staff and individual philanthropists giving $20,000 or more to Jewish and other causes. Contact: 15 E. 26th Street, Suite 1038, New York, NY 10010. Phone: 212/726-0177.

**Resourceful Women**—Provides financial and philanthropic education and personal support for women with wealth. Workshops, seminars and affinity groups address financial literacy, personal development, community activism and philanthropy. Coordinates the Women Donors Network—a national network of RW members who have annual philanthropic budgets of at least $25,000 and a commitment to progressive philanthropy. Members share strategies, experiences, vision, skills and creativity. Contact: Presidio Building #1016, P.O. Box 29423, San Francisco, CA 94129. Phone: 415/561-6520; E-mail: distaff@rw.org.

**Women's Philanthropy Institute**—Brings together philanthropists and philanthropy professionals to educate and advance women as major donors for the nonprofit causes of their choosing. Offers seminars, a quarterly newsletter, speaker training and a national speakers bureau. Contact: 1605 Monroe Street, Suite 105, Madison, WI 53711-2052. Phone: 608/286-0980; E-mail: andrea@women-philanthropy.org; Web site: www.women-philanthropy.org.

# Money Management

## BOOKS AND PUBLICATIONS

Janet Bamford, *et al. The Consumer Reports Money Book: How to Get it, Save it, and Spend it Wisely*. New York: Consumers Union, 1992.

Joe Dominguez and Vicki Robin, *Your Money or Your Life: Transforming Your Relationships with Money and Achieving Financial Independence*. New York: Viking Press, 1992.

*Taking Charge of Our Money, Our Values and Our Lives: Guide to 350 Publications and Organizations*. The Impact Project, 2244 Alder Street, Eugene, OR 97405. Phone: 541/343-2420; E-mail: impact@efn.org. Web site: www.efn.org.~impact.

Independent Sector, *How Much is Really Tax-deductible: A Basic Guide for Donors and Charitable Organizations*. 1997. Phone: 202/223-8100.

Peter Kinder, Steven Lydenberg, and Amy Domini, *Investing for Good: Making Money While Being Socially Responsible*. New York: HarperCollins, 1993.

Sally S. Kleberg, *The Stewardship of Private Wealth: Managing Personal and Family Financial Assets*. New York: McGraw-Hill, 1997.

Susan Meeker-Lowry, *Invested in the Common Good*. Philadelphia: New Society Press. 1995.

Jessie H. O'Neill, *The Golden Ghetto: The Psychology of Affluence*. Hazelden Publishing and Education., P.O. Box 176. Center City, MN 55012 0176. Phone: 800/328-0098. Web site: www.affluenza.com.

Suze Orman, *The 9 Steps to Financial Freedom*. New York: Crown Publishing Group, Inc, 1997.

Dan Rottenberg, *The Inheritors Handbook: A Definitive Guide for Beneficiaries*. Bloomberg Press, 1998.

Barbara Stanny, *Prince Charming Isn't Coming: How Women Get Smart about Money*. New York: Viking, 1997.

Deanne Stone and Barbara Block, *Choosing and Managing Financial Professionals*. San Francisco: Resourceful Women, 1994. Phone: 415/561-6520.

Letia Young, *Money Book for Young Adults, Ages 12-17*, and *Money Book for Kids, Ages 6-11*. 3478 Buskirk Avenue, Suite 1031, Pleasant Hill, CA 94523. Phone: 510/686-5518.

# Philanthropic Reform

**Business Leaders for Sensible Priorities**—Business owners, CEOs and corporate executives who are committed to increasing public investment in the common good that provide security to Americans: education, health care, the environment, and a secure future for senior citizens. Leaders are mobilized to redirect U.S. Federal budget priorities away from Cold War military expenditure levels and toward meeting the needs of society without increasing the deficit. Contact: 130 William Street, Suite 700, New York, NY 10038. Phone: 212/964-1109.

**Changemakers**—Works in collaboration with others to strengthen the infrastructure of progressive philanthropy. Contact: P.O. Box #428, Ross, CA 94957. Phone: 415/461-5539.

**Independent Sector**—Promotes philanthropy, volunteerism and research of the nonprofit sector. Contact: 1828 L Street NW, Suite 1200, Washington, D.C. 20036. Phone: 202/223-8100; E-mail: info@indepsec.org; Web site: www.indepsec.org.

**National Committee for Responsive Philanthropy**—Seeks through research and advocacy to make mainstream philanthropy more responsive to marginalized communities and progressive causes. Contact: 2001 S Street NW, #620, Washington, D.C. 20009. Phone: 202/387-9177; E-mail: ncrp@aol.com.

**United for a Fair Economy**—A national organization drawing public attention to the growth of income and wealth inequality in the U.S. and to the implications of this inequality for America's democracy, economy and society. Its project, Responsible Wealth, organizes persons of wealth to speak out for economic fairness. Quarterly newsletter and workshops. Contact: 37 Temple Place, 5th Floor, Boston, MA 02111. Phone: 617/423-2148; E-mail: stw@stw.org. Web site: www.stw.org.

# Index

*Page numbers in italics indicate exercises and worksheets.*

# About the Authors

**TRACY GARY**

Tracy Gary has been a donor activist and philanthropist for more than twenty-five years. She has been a founder of more than twelve nonprofits, including Resourceful Women, The Women's Foundation of San Francisco and the International Donor Dialogue Network.

Tracy supports and educates donors, family foundations, financial service organizations and nonprofits about the stewardship of money, leadership and philanthropy through Community Consulting Services.

Through her extensive public speaking and private consultations, Tracy has worked with groups as diverse as American Express Financial Services, The Institute of Noetic Sciences, regional grantmaking associations, planned giving and fundraising councils, alumni associations, private, family and community foundations, donor networks and grassroots community groups.

She can be reached by E-mail at tracygary1@aol.com, or by fax at (415) 925-9411.

**MELISSA KOHNER**

Photo: Jeanne Van Atta

Melissa Kohner has been active organizing young donors and leaders for eight years. She has worked with the political and financial concerns of donors (young and old) nationwide through individual and group consultation and workshops; she has been a speaker at conferences of organizations ranging from the Council on Foundations to the Women's Funding Network. She has worked in community economic development, fundraising and grantmaking and served on numerous grantmaking committees. Melissa is a board member of the National Network of Grantmakers and Third Wave Foundation.

Melissa can be reached by E-mail at msk4@aol.com, or by fax at (215) 247-7275.

# Resources for Social Change

## AVAILABLE FROM CHARDON PRESS...

publishing materials that help build a broad progressive movement for social justice

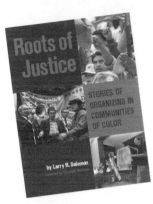

Keep up-to-date on new fundraising techniques and issues. Learn how to increase your income and diversify your sources of funding using proven, practical strategies, including special events, direct mail, major donor programs, membership campaigns and more. **$32/year; $58/2 years**

*Roots of Justice* recaptures some of the nearly forgotten histories of communities of color. These are the stories of people who fought back against exploitation and injustice — and won. It shows how, through organizing, ordinary people have made extraordinary contributions to change society. **$15**

Kim Klein's classic how-to fundraising text teaches you everything you need to know to raise money successfully from individuals. Learn how to motivate your board of directors; analyze your constituency; plan and implement major gifts campaigns, endowments and planned giving programs; use direct mail techniques successfully; and more. **$25**

An introduction to the most common and successful fundraising strategies in 14 of the best articles from the *Grassroots Fundraising Journal*. Small organizations can put these strategies to use immediately. This reprint collection in Spanish only. **$12**

### Bulk Discounts Available!

For more information about these and many other titles, contact us for a free catalog and visit our Web site at

### www.chardonpress.com

Veteran organizer Gary Delgado provides a compelling look at where organizing is going and how it's changing. Called by one reviewer, "The most important analysis of community organizing since the 1960's," this book is essential reading for anyone involved in grassroots organizations. **$25**

A model for linking grassroots organizing with political analysis and policy development. Using the issues of community safety and police accountability, *Justice by the People* shows how to link education with action—in 15 provocative and lively workshops. **$25**

A collection of readings for students and prospective jurors. *Juries* provides background about the realities of the police, court and penal systems relevant to jurors in criminal trials. Mara Taub, a teacher and community volunteer, introduces each chapter with comments about her own jury experience. **$15**

**CHARDON PRESS**
P.O. Box 11607, Berkeley, CA 94712
PHONE: (510) 704-8714
FAX: (510) 649-7913
E-MAIL: chardn @chardonpress.com

# ORDER FORM

## Grassroots Fundraising Journal

### SUBSCRIPTIONS
*Please allow 6 weeks for processing new subscriptions.*

**United States**
- ☐ 1 year @ $32 _____
- ☐ 2 years @ $58 _____
- ☐ 3 years @ $84 _____

**Canada & Overseas**
- ☐ 1 year @ $39 _____
- ☐ 2 years @ $65 _____
- ☐ 3 years @ $91 _____

**SUBTOTAL: $** _____

*There are no tax or shipping charges for subscriptions.*

### REPRINT COLLECTIONS*
- ☐ The Board of Directors  $10 _____
- ☐ Getting Major Gifts  $10 _____
- ☐ Cómo Recaudar Fondos…  $12 _____

*\* Please call for bulk discounts.*

### BACK ISSUES
- ☐ All Available Back Issues: $150 _____
- ☐ Individual Back Issues:  $5 each _____

*Single articles not available.*

| QUANTITY | VOLUME & NUMBER | COST |
|---|---|---|
| _____ | _____ | _____ |
| _____ | _____ | _____ |
| _____ | _____ | _____ |
| _____ | _____ | _____ |

**SUBTOTAL: $** _____

## Books

- ☐ **Fundraising for Social Change**
  *by Kim Klein*
  - ___ 1–4 copies @ $25 each _____
  - ___ 5–9 copies @ $20 each _____
  - ___ 10+ copies @ $15 each _____

- ☐ **Grassroots Grants** *by Andy Robinson*
  - ___ 1–4 copies @ $25 each _____
  - ___ 5–9 copies @ $20 each _____
  - ___ 10+ copies @ $15 each _____

- ☐ **Roots of Justice** *by Larry Salomon*
  - ___ copies @ $15 each _____

- ☐ **Juries: Conscience of the Community** *by Mara Taub*
  - ___ copies @ $17 each _____

- ☐ **Justice by the People**
  *by Terry Keleher/Applied Research Center*
  - ___ copies @ $25 each _____

- ☐ **Beyond the Politics of Place**
  *by Gary Delgado/Applied Research Center*
  - ___ copies @ $25 each _____

- ☐ **Inspired Philanthropy**
  *by Tracy Gary & Melissa Kohner*
  - ___ copies @ $20 each _____

**SUBTOTAL: $** _____

### SHIPPING/HANDLING CHARGES

| ORDER TOTALLING | SHIPPING FEE |
|---|---|
| $ 5.00 – 20.00 | $ 2.00 |
| $ 20.01 – 25.00 | $ 4.00 |
| $ 25.01 – 50.00 | $ 6.00 |
| $ 50.01 – 75.00 | $ 8.00 |
| $ 75.01 –100.00 | $10.00 |
| $100.01 or more | 10% of order |

- ☐ 2nd day air  + $5.00
- ☐ Overnight  + $10.00

**Overseas (including Canada & Mexico):**
For each shipping & handling level above, multiply by 2 (Payment in U.S. dollars only).

*Please allow 2–4 weeks for delivery.*

**Reprint Collections / Back Issues** *Subtotal:* $ _____ +
**Books** *Subtotal:* $ _____ = $ _____
In CA add 8.25% sales tax to above total: $ _____
Shipping & Handling (see chart above): $ _____
**SUBSCRIPTION** *Subtotal:* $ _____
**TOTAL AMOUNT ENCLOSED:** $ _____

Name _____

Organization _____

Address _____

City/State/Zip _____

Phone _____

### CREDIT CARD ORDERS
- ☐ MasterCard   ☐ VISA

Card #: _____

Expiration date: _____

Signature: _____

Please make checks payable to:
**CHARDON PRESS**

P.O. Box 11607
Berkeley, CA 94712

PHONE: (510) 704-8714

FAX: (510) 649-7913

E-MAIL:
chardn @chardonpress.com

WEB PAGE:
www.chardonpress.com

# Notes

# Notes

# Notes

# "Values" Cards

| ACCEPTANCE | BEAUTY | COMMITMENT | COMMUNICATION |
| COMMUNITY | COMPASSION | COURAGE | CREATIVITY |
| DEMOCRACY | DIGNITY | DIVERSITY | EQUALITY |
| FAITH | FAMILY | FREEDOM | HARMONY |
| HEALING | HONESTY | INTERDEPENDENCE | INTEGRITY |
| JUSTICE | JOY | KNOWLEDGE | LOVE |
| OPPORTUNITY | PEACE | PRESERVATION | RESPECT |
| RESPONSIBILITY | SERVICE | SIMPLICITY | TRANSFORMATION |

# "Issues and Populations" Cards

| | | | |
|---|---|---|---|
| AIDS | Animals | Anti-Semitism | Anti-Racism |
| Arts and Art Institutions | Boys | Catholic Charities | Children |
| Civil Rights | Community Gardens | Corporate Responsibility | Demilitarization |
| Disability Rights | Disaster Relief | Drug and Alcohol Abuse | Domestic Violence |
| Economic Justice | Education | Employment Training and Job Creation | Environment/ Environmental Justice |
| Electoral Reform | Faith-Based Community Service | Gay/Lesbian/ Bisexual Civil Rights | Girls |
| Gun Control | Healthcare and Medical Research | Homelessness/ Housing | Human Rights |
| Immigrant and Refugee Rights and Services | International Development | Jewish Causes | Legal Aid |

# "Issues and Populations" Cards

| | | | |
|---|---|---|---|
| Libraries | Media | Native and Indigenous Peoples' Rights | Parks and Land Preservation |
| Peace/ Conflict Resolution | Philanthropy and Volunteerism | Poverty | Prison Reform |
| Public Policy/ Advocacy | Reproductive Rights | Seniors | Spiritual Development |
| Sports | Sustainable Development | Women's Rights | Youth Development |